How To Get To The Top Of Google

Tim Kitchen
www.Get2TheTopOfGoogle.com

Table of Contents

Introduction

Who is this book for

This book will be most useful to the following groups of people:

- Small business owners
- Small business workers in charge of their internet presence
- Online businesses or businesses with an online component (e.g. wedding photographer who needs to be found online or who can sell photos online)
- SEO companies – both existing companies and freelancers thinking of starting their own SEO company. (For those who don't know, SEO is Search Engine Optimisation. SEOs or Search Engine Optimisers are often brought in by website owners to get their websites to rank highly on Google, and paid large amounts of money to do it. This book contains the secrets of what they do.)
- Bloggers who want their website to rank highly in order to get more traffic

In short, if you want to get a website to the top of Google, this book is what you need.
The strategies contained in it are not to be taken lightly.
You will find many simple fundamental rules that many business owners are breaking *without even knowing it*, and you'll learn small changes that can be made to cause a rocketing of ranking in Google.

But this book also contains some of the most advanced strategies in use today by the world's top SEO companies. These companies regularly charge thousands of dollars per month for implementing the very strategies you will read in this book. Nearly all major companies employ SEO specialists - whether internally or outsourced - to take charge of their SEO, because they understand how important being ranked highly on Google is.

What they don't understand is the tips, tricks and secrets these SEO companies actually use to deliver the sort of results they are able to charge tens or even hundreds of thousands (even *millions* in some cases) of dollars per year for.
In this book, you will be learning those very strategies and will see for yourself the impact they will have on your business.
I hope you are excited by the possibilities!
If you would like to contact me, my personal email is tim@exposureninja.com

Google's Panda & Penguin Updates

The SEO world has changed significantly in 2012, and April's Google Penguin update was the final nail in the coffin for many of the most widespread SEO techniques in use by those looking for fast results. Fear and panic spread through the industry as website rankings plummeted and many SEOs began to worry if their livelihoods were at stake now that many of their most common strategies were not only ineffective but actually *harmed* rankings.
We'll be looking at the effects of Google Penguin in more detail later on. But throughout this book I have included the results of my own testing and experience as I have continued to run my SEO-based businesses, post-Penguin.

And of course we'll be looking at how you can get results whilst staying safe and avoiding penalties.

Why this book exists

This book exists because I grew fed up seeing and hearing about companies charging website owners who could barely afford it £200+ per month to do essentially very simple things. I thought that businesses who couldn't afford these outrageous fees deserved the same results.
In short, I saw Google becoming like the Yellow Pages used to be: the big companies with big marketing budgets could afford to get top positions, whereas the little guys were forced onto page 2 or 3 if they were lucky, but more likely pages 10 and beyond. And if you're not on the first couple pages at least, you might as well be invisible.
Once the little guys were forced off page 1, their business dropped and they began to struggle. It's a vicious cycle that ends very badly for those who don't have the cash to compete. And I don't think that's right.

The 3 'Dirty Secrets' Expensive SEO Companies Don't Want You To Know

1) You are more than capable of doing your own SEO. Once you understand *what* to do, actually doing it is quite straightforward and mostly about performing quite repetitive tasks. Many SEO companies actually outsource or automate a lot of this stuff, which is why they try to hide their 'secrets' to justify sky-high prices.
2) You understand your market better than an SEO company will. Therefore you are best placed to identify what your customers want, where they hang out online, and what about you appeals to them. You are best positioned to promote your website, so taking the time to learn how to do it is extremely important.
3) Many of the companies that might call you up on the phone offering to get you to the top of Google call themselves SEO companies, but actually just outsource the whole lot and charge you a fat commission. With the information in this book, you will be better placed to learn exactly what they do, so that next time someone tries to pitch you for SEO services you can judge for yourself whether or what they are offering is worth the high fee. Of course, once you have read this book you can implement all the strategies that they are outsourcing yourself, for free, right now.

The Internet As A Level Playing Field

As I mentioned before, one of the best things about Google and the internet in general is that it is supposed to offer a level playing field: the small companies can compete with the large companies on the same Google results page. This is the beauty of the Internet, and I believe this is how it should be - free and equal, not an auction where the big players get bigger and the small fish starve to death.

The emerging inequality that I saw unfolding means that the big players have access to the tips, tricks and secrets because they can afford the experts to do the work for them. These experts hold their secrets close to their chests and don't publicise their techniques for fear of breeding more competition and losing their competitive edge.

This is all well and good, but what about the smaller companies who have smaller (or perhaps no) online marketing budget?

In the interests of keeping the Internet a level playing field, I decided that these techniques, tricks and strategies needed to be shared. Everyone deserves access to the strategies that get proven results, whether they have money to spend or not.

That's where this book comes in. As well as being a comprehensive guide, it's an 'expose' on the SEO industry: the tricks and techniques that work as well as some new secret strategies that even the bigger players aren't using yet. All are presented here for you in one place, with clear instructions to give beginners and experienced SEOs (Search Engine Optimisers) the tools to get to the first page or top result in Google.

My Background

To give a bit of background on me, I have set up, run and been in charge of SEO for various internet businesses over the past 8 years. For each and every one, getting prime position on Google was absolutely critical to their success. Some of my businesses I started in areas that didn't previously exist, so getting to the top of Google was relatively easy and it was all about maintaining that position once the competition started flooding the market. Some of my other businesses fought fierce competition with local rivals however, and beating them in the 'Google Shootout' was a lot more hard-fought initially. You will see and hear about examples of both sorts throughout this book.

I have lost count of the number of websites I have built (well over 100), domains bought and hours spent doing, testing and researching SEO (I don't even want to think about it!).

The end result is that I know what I'm talking about. For me, first place on Google isn't a 'nice idea' or wish, it's a part of daily life.

I don't say this to brag, I just want you to know that this stuff comes from testing, measuring and experience, not regurgitation.

I now run Exposure Ninja, an online marketing, web design and SEO company, and Job Done Websites which promotes tradesmen online.

Since Google Penguin, the amount of misinformation and conjecture regarding what works and what doesn't has exploded. As soon as 2 weeks after the Penguin update was released, a flood of blogs, books and videos appeared announcing 'the latest Penguin-safe SEO strategies'. In my opinion, the reality is that 2 weeks (or even 2 months) is nowhere near enough time to evaluate a new or existing strategy's effectiveness or gather enough data to be sure about a hypothesis. Beware of the wizard.

How to use this book

There is a lot of content here. Some of the tips, tricks and strategies in this book represent years of research and take many hours to implement. Others are quick and easy tricks you can do today to get fast results.

My advice is to cherry pick the strategies that suit you. Do the ones which are most relevant to you (although the strategies in here can be used by almost any business or personal website), and which fit in with your daily life.

However, be aware that some strategies have a bigger effect than others on your Google rank. Bear in mind that if the thought of putting that amount of time into a certain task puts you off, you are not alone. That is *exactly* what your competition would say. That bears repeating: if the thought of putting that amount of time into a certain task puts you off, you are not alone. That is *exactly* what your competition would say.

Then it becomes about how much you really want this and if you are willing to invest the time and effort necessary. By getting this book you are off to a very good start.

I would recommend that you read about each and every strategy, whether you plan to implement it or not. It's helpful to know about the tools in your arsenal, even if you don't intend to use them. You will also be able to spot these techniques in action while you are surfing the Internet, and it will give you a new appreciation of some of the best websites and online promotional campaigns.

If you are a freelance Search Engine Optimiser or run an SEO company, again you will want to know and understand all of the strategies in this book even if you don't intend to use them. Should you find yourself working with a client in a particularly competitive niche it will be helpful to have some 'heavy firepower' to back you up and give you the edge against the competition.

If you are a small business and your competitors are employing a dedicated SEO company, you will be forced to do more work to compete (for advice on how to check what your competitors are up to, read on). But please understand - just because they are employing an expensive company doesn't mean you can't beat them. They are using the same techniques you will learn about in this book and with your specialist understanding of your market and your customers, you are actually in a stronger position than an SEO company to achieve fantastic results.

The Sad Truth About Most Websites

The sad truth about most websites is that they don't think about SEO. If they are on the front page of Google it is by happy accident. If this sounds true for your market then you are in luck because, as the saying goes, 'in the land of the blind, the one-eyed man is king'. If your competition is relatively 'blind' when it comes to search engine optimization, you are in for a treat because whatever you do your efforts will have a far greater effect on your Google ranking than others who are in a more competitive market.

The Structure of the Book

First we will look at Google, the world's most popular search engine. As the title of this book suggests, we will be focusing solely on 'the big G' throughout. However, the strategies in this book work equally well for other search engines including Yahoo, Microsoft's Bing, AOL (which now uses Google search) and the hapless, dead in the water Ask.com.

The trend that we've been seeing over the past decade is Google's increasing dominance while other search engines are left in the dust. There is good reason for this, as Google is at the cutting edge of search technology and works extremely hard to make its search the most accurate and useful search engine on the planet.

It is worth keeping this in mind when we being talking about Google's updates: any updates Google implements which affect how it displays search results have the aim of keeping its position as number one. This is a GOOD THING for us, even though it might not feel like it at the time. Each time there is a Google update, some websites are penalized while others receive a boost in the rankings. There is simultaneous outcry and joy expressed across the world's online forums. As we will see later on, the best long-term tactic for good Google ranking is to be legitimate, honest and strictly above-board when optimizing and promoting our website. Google just wants the best for its users (the searchers, that is) so as long as we keep *the searchers* happy, Google will continue to reward us with good ranking.

This has never been truer than with Panda and Penguin. The techniques that Google penalized sites for using weren't chosen randomly or haphazardly, but instead they are the techniques that clearly identify a less-than-savoury approach favouring spam methods over real human-focussed promotion.

After looking at Google, we will take a look at our own website and how to make it 'Google Friendly' as well as 'visitor friendly'. Always remember that your website is built to generate customers or readers for you or your business. Never sacrifice that aim in order to get good Google ranking. Being at the top of Google is pointless if your website doesn't lead to more happy visitors.

The third section of the book looks at promoting your website around the Internet. This is absolutely crucial to Google ranking and constitutes the majority of ongoing work that you will need to do in order to get and maintain top position on Google.

Finally we will look at piecing together a strategy for you to follow for your website's Google dominance. You will see examples of my own strategies for getting websites to the top of Google, and as always you are encouraged to 'swipe at will' and use for your own website.

Throughout the book I will be addressing some of the most common myths surrounding Google ranking; myths that many people waste significant amounts of time on (perhaps including your competitors) even though they have little or no effect on Google ranking.

For efficiency's sake, from now on I will be assuming that you are a business, and the purpose of your website is to attract customers. Whether you are an SEO company, SEO freelancer or you run an information website like a blog, the principles are exactly the same even if your website visitors do not pay you or you are promoting websites on behalf of others.

Case Study: Ben Mullins of TivertonPlastering.com

Ben was my neighbor while I was living in Tiverton, Devon. A plasterer by trade, I got talking to him one day and obviously, doing what I do, asked him if he attracted much work from the Internet. He mentioned that he had spent £1,800 paying a website company to build him a website but it had never materialized, they stopped returning his calls and the experience with being ripped off had put him off getting involved with the internet since.

It frustrates me when people have a negative image of the net based on these horror stories. Not because I think it's wrong - they're right to be skeptical - but because a few bad apples have spoiled the barrel for many web design companies out there.

So I offered to build Ben a website, and promote it, and we could see what happens. Part of me wanted to try out some ideas from what I'd learnt building and promoting other sites, and take it to a local business like Ben's in a really rural area. This would be a perfect experimental opportunity.

Plus I could see that he was around quite a lot of the day and he said work had been pretty slow recently.

So I built him a website, registered him with Google Places (more about that later on) and took out some Google ads. The website didn't take long to build and, unusually for me, I didn't do very much research into his market - a scene I didn't know much about at that point. I got on with my other work and it slipped to the back of my mind.

Anyway, a week or so later Ben called to say he'd had a few nice jobs from the website already, despite not actually having seen it himself yet (he doesn't have his own computer). So I started promoting the site a little bit, wondering what would happen if he got to the top of Google. Would those few jobs from the Google ads turn into a steady stream of work?

Getting to the top of Google isn't easy. The process is straightforward, but I wouldn't say it's *easy* like riding a bike is easy or counting to 10 is easy.

For one thing, it takes time. How long it takes depends on a number of factors including the level of competition and how long Google takes before they index your site.

I saw Ben from time to time and he mentioned that the site was bringing him some work, and this was cool but I was doing other stuff and it didn't really occur to me to push it. Then I moved away.

A couple months later (it was a Friday night I think) and my phone rang. It was Ben. What he had to say completely knocked me sideways.

In the last month or so, the amount of work he'd got had rocketed. He was so busy he now had 5 or 6 guys working for him, doing the jobs he was too busy to do! A huge local contract had just come through, and for the first time he was now *turning work away*. Whereas before he had been asking more established plasterers for work, they were now the ones coming to him asking for work.

What had happened, I wondered?

"It's the website" he said. "Everyone has found me on the internet". I grabbed my laptop, flipped open the lid and, with the phone under my ear quickly typed "tiverton plastering" to see where he was showing up.

Sure enough, Google had indexed his site and he was now at the top of Google.

He couldn't stop praising the website and the Internet and how it had completely transformed his business: from being bottom of the heap in his town to being the top dog in four months.

All thanks to a simple website and being top of Google.

Hmm, I thought. Looks like the experiment worked.

The next weekend I drove back to Tiverton to meet up with him to find out more (and get his excitement on film. You cannot waste this sort of testimonial!). As I got to his house I could see all his plastering gear in the driveway. What was he doing, I asked.

"Got this huge job starting tomorrow at a local factory. Just getting all my stuff ready."

After chatting for 5 minutes, the change in his behavior was striking. Whereas before he was quiet and gave of an almost withdrawn or suspicious vibe, he was now full of confidence, leading the conversation and seemed to have a spark about him that just wasn't there when we first met. He even said how the amount of work he had been getting had boosted his confidence to an extent where he was now charging higher prices than his competitors, and still getting the job!

Over the course of our chat he mentioned that he was now in a position where he and his partner had discussed her leaving her job (she worked night shifts so they didn't get to spend much time together), and he was also starting to consider buying his own house.

I'll be honest - this floored me.

Of course, I knew the power of being top of Google from my own online businesses, but this was the first time I had seen the effect of these strategies on *someone else's* business.

And the results were clear to see.

I drove home that evening with my mind buzzing. How could I get this stuff out there to other offline businesses? It was an opportunity too good to waste.

So I started building and promoting websites for other tradesmen. Sure enough, the strategies that I had used to promote my own websites were working for their websites too!

But I knew this stuff had to get out there faster than I could do the work myself.

Hence this book was born. As a direct result from seeing the impact that getting good Google ranking can have on <u>any</u> business - big or small, online or offline. I hope what it contains has the effect on you and your business that it has had for Ben and his.

Google

What Being at the Top Of Google Will Mean For Your Business

Because you are reading this book, I don't need to tell you how important Google is to people whether they are looking for information or looking to buy something online.

For most people, Google is one of their most visited websites. In fact it might have been recently overtaken by Facebook as the world's most visited website, but that doesn't make its impact any less significant.

When your customers look for a product or service - your product or service - online, they use Google most of the time. In the UK, Google is the main search engine for 90% of the population. What I can also tell you having studied the analytics for my own websites, is that the vast, *vast* majority of all traffic to your website will be from Google rather than any of the other search engines.

For many businesses, being on the first page of Google is enough to sustain them with virtually no other marketing. It's the equivalent effect that a big Yellow Pages advert had 15 years ago. Enough prospective customers are out there looking for that product or service that just being found on Google is enough to feed a high-ranking business a steady stream of customers.

While this might seem like an ideal position, and certainly many of the businesses in this position are extremely happy to be there, it can also be dangerous. Being at the mercy of Google ranking can be costly if that rank suddenly drops - and it can if you're not careful.

There are countless stories of websites that have relied on dodgy techniques, or forbidden 'black hat' strategies being top position one day and completely disappearing the next after the latest Google update.

You can insulate yourself against this danger by carrying out good SEO and making sure you stay on the right side of the black hat/white hat line, which we will cover in more detail later on.

But it is undeniable that first page Google rank is seen by many as the Holy Grail, and top position is rightly coveted very preciously.

The numbers quoted vary from different sources, but the most recent figures I have seen from 2011 suggest that the first 'organic' result of the first page in Google gets between 36% and 56% of all the clicks on the page. This is a phenomenally high figure, and the resulting impact on your business is obvious, particularly if you're not currently showing up on Google at all!

Imagine immediately siphoning off 36%-56% of your competition's visitors! It's really no wonder that being the first result is so prized.

(Later on I will give you more advanced strategies for dominating the Google results page, including one example where I was able to grab 6 of the first 7 results!)

Having stressed the importance of first position, I also want to remind you that appearing *anywhere* on the first page is better than being lost in the dark depths of pages 2 and beyond (with one exception: a 2011 study showed that being ranked first on page 2 actually got more clicks than being ranked 10th on page 1. But that's the exception).

So as a rule, page 1 equals good. Page 2 or worse equals bad.

Implied Expertise

One significant effect of being ranked first in Google is the implied expertise. The general public doesn't understand what it takes to be first in Google, which is why first position is so popular. If they knew that the sites were ranked according which website was best optimized and had the highest Pagerank (we will look at Pagerank later on), they might dig a little deeper.

The result is that many of the general public simply assume that the top result in Google is, generally, 'the best' and they place their trust in Google to serve them the best result.

The top result might have shoddy customer service, high prices, and be employing slave labour, but Google doesn't care - or rather Google *has no way to track this.* All Google wants to do is serve the most relevant results to its searchers.

In other words, if you want to appear the best option in your field, you need to be top of Google.

As I mentioned previously, the beauty of Google is that, to an extent, it offers a level playing field. On the whole, little boutique shops can compete with large chain shops. Small gyms fight it out with large chain gyms. Independent home hair stylists can compete with the established chains, all on the same Google results page.

This of course assumes that both the big company and the little company are focused on SEO. Often, the little companies are too busy to invest the time necessary to compete and so never get to experience the level playing field in action.

But the potential is there for everyone to compete in the same arena. This book and the strategies in it are my attempt to share the secrets used by the big players to give smaller players the clout to do just that.

The 3 Ways to Show Up On Google

On Google there are 3 different places you can show up on the first page.

What most people tend to focus on is the 'organic' Google listings. These are the main results that show up on the middle of the page with a white background. This area is called organic, because it is not paid for. The sites are positioned there through a number of factors which we will look at in a minute.

The next way to show up on the front page of Google is by advertising. Google's Adwords program means that website owners can pay to show up on the right hand side of the page, or right at the top in the yellow box. This might seem like a nice shortcut to getting on the front page, but the vast majority of web surfers are heavily conditioned to avoid adverts and although these ads are shown right at the top of the page, in total Adwords ads only get around 20% of the clicks on the page.

The third way to show up on the front page is through Google Places or Maps. Places has now been around for a while, and we're starting to see Google give more screen space to their maps listings than ever before as it becomes more popular amongst businesses that rely on a local presence or physical location. One of my clients is competing in a search that has only 3 organic listings on the first page, with the rest of the space being given to Google maps listings. This trend is likely to continue, and it emphasizes the importance of being in that top 3, as well as showing up on the map.

If your website is for a local business, you *need* to be on Google Places (now called Google+ Local). In fact, you might already be, (Google has already created listings for many established businesses) in which case it is important that you claim your listing as soon as possible and get to work optimizing it.

How to get good placement in Google Places/Google+ Local is beyond the scope of this book, but if this is of interest to you then you might like to check out my Kindle book "How to Get to The Top of Google Places / Google+ Local.

The Google Leapfrog – Using Video To Leapfrog Pages of Your Competitors

There's actually a fourth way to show up on the first page of Google, which is relatively under-used. Google likes video, and a nice little trick that you can use to literally leapfrog pages and pages of your competitors is to get a short promo video showing up right on the front page. We'll be looking at exactly how you can do this, and for very little effort, later on. .

How Google Decides Where To Rank You

The big question: how does Google decide who is at the top and who is second?

The answer is in the complex and secret algorithms they use to measure, amongst other things, a website's:

- Relevance to what the searcher is looking for
- Popularity of the site
- Size and profile
- Happy user experience – for example no broken links or missing pages

Relevance

If Google's search strategy could be summed up in one word, it would be relevance.

All Google's success to date has arguably come from its ability to serve up the most relevant results. A quick search on one of the other search engines (with the exception of AOL and others who actually use Google's search) demonstrates how easy it is to take for granted the relevance of Google results. If there's one thing that determines whether web users stick with their favourite search engine or decide to switch, it's relevance.

So how does Google measure relevance?

There are a huge number of ways and we will briefly look at them now before drilling down in more detail later on throughout this book.

Top of the list is, unsurprisingly, the content of your website. That is the words and, to some extent, the pictures. Google has software that is affectionately called 'robots' indexing the Internet constantly. These robots are crawling over your site, through all the pages and making a note each time particular phrases come up.

Myth Buster: indexing does not mean 'saving' your entire website, and Google doesn't store your whole website, but rather instances of particular words.

Myth Buster: Google doesn't index every single page. There are a huge number of web pages out there that get no visitors or attention and which Google doesn't bother indexing. It skips these pages because it prefers to focus on the websites it considers more important, namely those that are being updated and getting more traffic. The bad news is that if your pages aren't indexed, you aren't going to be showing up in the search results. So getting indexed is a top priority and we'll look at ways to encourage Google to index your web pages later on.

Traffic

While there is no concrete proof (because no one from Google has confirmed either way) it's a fairly safe bet that websites that attract the most clicks from Google tend to move up in the rankings.

It makes logical sense if you remember that Google wants to present the most relevant websites to its visitors. If lots of people click on site B even though it ranks below site A, then Google would see site B as being more relevant to its users and should move it up the rankings.

We know that Google measures the number of people that click on its adverts (this is called the Click Through Rate, or CTR) and the CTR affects the position of these adverts, so it makes sense that it would also affect the position of the regular listings too.

Pagerank

Pagerank is essentially what makes Google so special. Pagerank is a way to measure how popular a website is compared to all the other sites on the internet.
It measures this popularity by looking at the number and quality of links that point to it. So if lots of links point to web page A, but no links point to web page B, then web page A usually has a higher Pagerank. Incidentally the 'Page' in Pagerank has nothing to do with the web*page* but is named after Larry Page, a Google co founder, who thought up the mathematical algorithm to measure it.
So the number of links to a webpage is important but so is the *quality* (and Pagerank) of the website that the link comes from. This makes total sense if we think of an example:
My website gets a link from low quality blog comment whereas your website gets a link from the Harvard University homepage (Google particularly likes .edu addresses because they are less susceptible to being taken over by spammers). Which link means more? Obviously your link coming from a big recognized institution. This is reflected in the Pagerank which the links give our respected sites: your site would gain more Pagerank than mine in this example.
Pagerank flows through the links, so Harvard's website (which would have high Pagerank because so many other websites link to it) would pass Pagerank to your site. The low quality blog that linked to my site would have much less Pagerank, so would have less to pass on.
To make matters slightly more complicated, a page doesn't *lose* page rank when it passes Pagerank to another page. Also, the Pagerank it passes on is shared between all of the links on that page.
For example: let's say that your web page was the only link on the Harvard homepage. Unlikely, but if we use this example you will receive a *ton* of Pagerank for this because Harvard is basically saying, "this web page is the real deal. You have *got* to see this".

If on the other hand there were hundreds of links on the Harvard homepage and yours was only one of them, the Pagerank that gets passed along would be shared by all the links on that page.
The only way to 'create' Pagerank is to create a new page. Each page is born with Pagerank, and shares this Pagerank with all the pages that it links to.
This means that bigger websites - websites with more pages - naturally have the opportunity to get a higher Pagerank, because all the smaller pages can feed back into the homepage and really boost its score.
We're going to be looking shortly at why you should build lots of pages on your website and what you should be filling them with, but for now think of lots of pages in orbit around your homepage all feeding Pagerank to it.
Let's leave Pagerank there, we will briefly revisit it when we talk about links later on but for now remember that Pagerank is Google's measure of importance. And the Pagerank of a page has a huge effect on where it shows up in the Google listings.
We will also talk about the importance of relevance when choosing which websites to get links from.

Keywords

We mentioned that Google's robots crawl your webpages and make a note of words that are found on them. When someone types in a phrase, Google scans its memory of the Internet for instances of the words in that phrase.
Where they are found, up pops the page.
The things people type into Google to find your product or service are called keywords. For example "plumber in London", "diet plans" or "how to get to the top of Google".

These keywords are extremely important when building and optimizing your website and you will become extremely familiar with your particular keywords by the time your website is top of Google!

Every page of your website that is supposed to attract visitors (i.e. not privacy policy or other boring pages like that) should be built around and optimized for certain keywords.

The keywords that you decide on will depend on your business, your particular service or product, your competition and the habits of your customers.

And just to be 100% clear, you can (and should) build different pages with different keywords in mind. Your homepage isn't the only page that can show up in Google and having lots of different pages (focused on lots of different keywords) means you have lots of different options all fighting for position and that's what can lead to double, triple and even quadruple listings on the first page of Google (as I will show you later).

Here's an exercise: write down what your customers and potential customers type into Google if they want to find the thing that you sell. This is the most important exercise you can to in preparation of your SEO campaign.

The most common mistake people make is assuming that their potential customers are typing in their business name: e.g "Hair by Sarah" rather than the category "hair salon Essex" or even the problem they need solved "wedding hair cuts". I am constantly approached by clients who want to rank well in Google for their business name. While this is extremely easy to do and would be very easy money, I always try to help them see that the way to attracting *new* customers is to show up in front of people who are searching for what you do, even if they've never heard of you before.

Do your customers *really* search for you specifically by name? Do they even search for your product, or do they search for what it does for them?

Another example: Pete runs Pete's Autos, a car mechanics in Croydon.

His regular customers might type in "Pete's Autos Croydon", but these guys are probably going to find Pete whatever happens - they want Pete's and only Pete's. So Pete doesn't need to put too much effort into SEO'ing his site to show up for this.

It's the customers typing in "car mechanic Croydon" or even "new clutch Croydon" that represent extra new business for Pete, so these are the keywords Pete should be writing on his list.

So list each of your main products and services - in the language of your customers (so Pete's Mega Service Package is "car servicing" or "car service and valet" for example). Then under each product or service, identify the problems it solves and the benefits it provides. If you are a business that targets a specific location, then add the location to your list too.

Hopefully you should have a big long list. From this list, eliminate any phrases that are too generic ("feel good" as a benefit for Sarah's Wedding Hair Service, for example) and you should be left with a list of keywords that your future customers will be typing to find you.

Let's see what some of Pete's Keywords might be:

- Car mechanic Croydon
- Car repair Croydon
- New clutch Croydon
- MOT Croydon
- Wheel alignment Croydon
- Car servicing Croydon
- VW repair Croydon
- etc

Keep your list of keywords handy because we're going to be using them later on.

Analysing Your Competition & Identifying their Strengths and Weaknesses

Now we have a list of suitable keywords, it's time to analyse your competition. It's important to know what you're up against for a couple reasons:

1) Savvy competitors can save you work by showing you what you should be doing – all you need to do is copy them and do more of the same
2) Less savvy competitors can highlight serious gaps in their approach which you can use to your advantage and leap frog them in the Google rankings

Let's start right at the beginning. Go to Google and search for your main keyword. This will be your business category or main service, e.g. "book store" with a local area if you are a local business. E.g "business networking in Gloucester." Don't panic about where you show up, we're focusing on your competition here:

- Make a note of who is top of the listings
- Who is second and so on
- Notice if any of your competitors are showing up more than once
- Are there a lot of Google adverts for this keyword?
- Are any of your competitors using these adverts?
- What does Google suggest as related searches? Could some of these be added to your keywords list?
- Are the sites that show up mostly directories or real businesses?

If you are a local business, as well as the above:

- Notice who is showing up on the map
- How many map results show up for that phrase?
- Is the map at the top of the search results, further down, or mixed in with the normal Google results?

Once you've absorbed all the information from this page, choose your second main keyword. This would be an alternative phrase that someone looking for your product or service might type, or a second service that you offer. Again, if you're local then use the local area name in your search too.

- Does the same competitor show up in top position for this search as for the last search?
- How many of the positions for this keyword are taken by competitors that showed up in the previous search?
- Are the same companies advertising as before?

I usually repeat this exercise with my 5 top keywords. The point of this is to really understand which companies are my main online competition for Google's top spot. If 5 different websites are coming top for my keywords, that means I have a different competitor for each top spot, so I'll be studying each of their strategies for each keyword.

However, if one website is consistently in first place for all the keywords, it usually means they really know what they're doing and have put a lot of work into this. I say *usually* - if it's a small niche or area it could just be pure luck. Either way, we're going to be giving them a nasty surprise later on when we overtake them.

The next thing I do is identify 3 main online competitors. Note that if you're a local business, these might not be your local competition but rather the websites that are coming up top in your searches the most often. They could be big chains or online retailers, or simply websites offering information about that particular market.

It's also a possibility that if you're in a competitive market, there will be more than 3 main competitors. If this is the case, I usually just pick the 3 biggest ones and write them down.

Of course if you're a small local cake shop, or another niche whose members aren't necessarily associated with aggressive Internet presences, it might be the case that you don't actually have 3 competitors online. In which case, be thankful and write as many as you have.

We're now going to forensically study their websites and find out how they got to number one so we can beat them.

Pick the number one competitor.

Search for the keyword that makes them rank highly and this time we're going to have a look at what shows up in the search results. Notice the title of their listing. Does it contain the keyword you searched for, or words from the phrase? Is it short or is it so long that Google has cut it short?

Now look at the description underneath the title of their listing. How many times do the keywords show up in the description? Does it read like normal writing or is it all broken up like this:

"plumber, plumbing, new boiler, boiler replacement in Surrey. Local plumber, plumbing services…" etc

Seeing this sort of thing is a sure sign that the site has been built or modified with SEO in mind, and 'over-SEOd'. This happens when the website owner gets too carried away with trying to rank highly on Google and forgets that their website should be built for people, not just search engines. The website might rank highly, but people will stop clicking on the site because what shows up in the search results looks so junky. What's more, since the recent Google updates, seeing this sort of thing in the search results has become less frequent as sites employing these techniques have lost ranking or Google has begun to ignore this spammy overuse of keywords.

Notice what sort of titles and descriptions you can see on the page: the results page contains a huge amount of information relevant to our mission so it's worth spending some more time noticing which descriptions and titles stand out or make you want to click on the link – we can borrow from these enticing titles and descriptions later on.

Once you've made a mental note of your main target's description and titles in the results page, it's time to click on the link to their site.

Notice which page opens when you click on the link – is it the homepage: e.g. www.petesmechanics.com or is it a different page, e.g. www.petesmechanics.com/mots-in-croydon?
On the best SEO'd sites, you'll notice that the address of the page that opens contains the keywords you searched for. In the example above, you'll see that the page petesmechanics.com/mots-in-croydon contains the words "MOTs" 'In" and "Croydon".
This is good practice and we'll be focusing on how to do this later on.
It also means that in all likelihood, this page has been specifically set up to show up for the keywords "MOTs in Croydon".
Next we're going to have a look to see how many times the phrase you initially searched for shows up on this web page.
Press CTRL+F if you're on a PC or cmd+F if you're on a mac, and type in the phrase you searched for.
You'll see how many times the keywords have been used on the page. This number might be anything from 0 on very poorly SEO'd sites to 30+ on over-SEO'd sites. In all likelihood, it will be somewhere in the middle.
Next, find how many times the individual words in the phrase appear, and also any variations, for example "roofer", "roofing", "roof". Google can read these variations and knows that they refer to the same thing, and it's a good idea to include keyword variations on your page. Notice if your competitors have done it.
The next thing we are going to do is look under the hood of your competitor's site, and see the code they used in this page. Sometimes they will have left tell tale signs of their strategy which we can borrow.
Right click on the side of the page, away from the text and pictures and click View Source, View Page Source or the similar option.
What will open will be a page of the code that the site is built from.
We are looking for a couple of sections in particular.

The first is a line that begins: `<meta name="keywords`...
If this line exists, then the website owner has at least attempted to optimise their website to show up on Google. If you look further along in the line, you'll see the list of keywords they have chosen to target with their website.

Whilst you shouldn't assume that they have got the 'right' list, it can be really helpful to see which keywords they've chosen and there might be one or two that you hadn't thought of. The point of all this research is just to absorb what your competitors are doing before we decide where to attack.

The next section we're going to look at starts `<title>`. What follows this `<title>` tag is the title of the page that showed up in the Google search. It's worth looking through this title to see how many times they have used the keyword you searched for.

If the title doesn't contain the keyword or phrase, this is good news because it can be an indication that their site is not properly optimised.

Now find the `<meta name="description"` section. If you can't find it, again that can mean that the site is under-optimised and this is great news.

But for most websites that have even been casually optimised, the `<meta name="description"` section will contain a brief description of the webpage. This description used to be what shows up in the Google search results, although Google tends nowadays to choose what text to display in search results from all the readable text on the web page itself.

This meta description can still give us some insight into the SEO techniques of your competitors though so notice how long it is and whether it makes sense or is just a long string of keywords.

What some people will do is stuff their meta description full of keywords, thinking this will get them more traffic from Google. What they don't think about is if potential visitors see this gibberish on the Google results page they are unlikely to click on that website!

Close the source code, and head back to the website.

The next thing you are going to do is look at the other pages on the website – but first, notice the links you can see on the page you landed on from Google. Are there lots of links to pages with juicy titles that contain some of your keywords, or are there only links to things like 'Contact' 'Privacy Policy' and 'About Us'?

It's generally good practice to have a separate page set up especially for each of your main keywords. This page will the keyword in the title, and the page address should contain the keyword. Then on that page, the keyword should be found plenty of times with any variations and modifiers. (Variations are obviously different forms of the same word: roofer, roofing, roof. Modifiers are what we call 'add on' words – so for example for the keyword: plumber, one modifier might be 'emergency' as in 'emergency plumber'.)

Try to notice if your competitors have plenty of different pages all focussed on different keywords.

They might not be linked to from the main navigation section and you might have to dig a little deeper to find them.

What many people do is hide the links to these pages at the bottom of their website in the footer. The reason they do this is they don't want to clutter the overall look of their website will links to dozens of pages, so they effectively 'sweep them under the carpet' and bury them right at the bottom out of sight.

It's your job as an SEO detective to find them, wherever they are hiding!

It's worth noting that this technique is becoming less popular as it is seen as spammy, and I'd strongly recommend avoiding it to be on the safe side of future Google updates.

Once you are satisfied that you have mentally logged all the different pages on your competitor's site, noticed which keywords they seem to be shooting for, seen how many times the term you searched for shows up on their page, you can move on to your next competitor.

This might seem like a lot of work, but trust me – this is a major shortcut to years of trial and error!

Backlinks

Remember that Google likes sites that have a lot of links pointing at them (these incoming links are called 'backlinks'). I'm going to show you how to find out how popular yours and your competitor's sites are on the net in terms of how many backlinks point at them.

There's a really easy way to do this, which although not as accurate as we'd like, is fine for getting an overall picture of what's going on in the world of backlinks.

Head over to www.backlinfinder.com and put in your website's address. The tool will search the major search engines to see how many backlinks to your site they have indexed. The problem with this is that Google isn't super-accurate about declaring how many backlinks it has stored for some reason, but, as I say, this method is fine for broad strokes comparisons. Backlink Finder will also show you how many pages of your site have been indexed, and what your site's Pagerank is.

Remember to check both the www.domain.com and domain.com (without the www.) versions of your website as these are seen as completely separate sites to most of the Internet.

Next, put your competitors' website addresses into the backlink finder and see how many backlinks *they* have indexed. You'll probably find that if they are ahead of you on Google, they have a lot more backlinks, higher Pagerank and more pages indexed.

If they have a lot of backlinks, you can head over to www.backlinkwatch.com which will list all of the backlinks they are currently receiving as well as the anchor text used in each link.

Anchor Text

Anchor text is the text used in a link. So when you're surfing on the net, you might see a word in blue underlined, something like click here. Obviously clicking on that link won't take you to somewhere called 'click here', those words are what we call the anchor text.

Why is anchor text important to understand?

The reason we love anchor text is because it identifies the webpage on the other end of the link with the words used in the anchor text. For example, in the 'click here' example, Google would see the worlds 'click here' and associate the page being linked to with the phrase 'click here'.

Hopefully you can also see that using 'click here' as anchor text is not the best idea in the world.

A far better idea is to use your keywords as anchor text, for example vintage furniture for a site that sells vintage furniture. This means that rather than 'click here', Google is associating the website with vintage furniture. This is another positive vote for your website in Google's eyes.

If, when you're looking at your competitor's backlinks in the backlinkwatch tool, you notice that they always have the same backlink text, take notice because this is likely the phrase they have singled out above all others to rank highly for.

Incidentally, one of the key characteristics of the Penguin update was that websites with the same phrase as anchor text for lots of links saw their ranking drop.

When building links then, it's a good idea to aim for anchor text diversity for your links, or Google might think that you've spammed your link out into the world and treat it as duplicate content. We'll cover this in more detail later on.

By now you should have a list of the keywords you plan to target and a list of your top competitors for those keywords.

You will have studied their websites and noticed the keywords they are targeting, and how aggressively they are targeting them by making a mental note of the frequency of those keywords on the page, in links and in the meta description and `<title>` tags, as well as the meta keywords section.

Phew!

Website structure

Before we leave your competitors' sites, we're just going to take a quick look at the structure of their websites.

By structure, we mean how the pages are ordered. Most well designed websites have pages at different 'levels'. For example top-level pages might be called Home, Contact, Services, Products etc. These pages are then might have pages underneath them (second-level pages) which go into more detail. For example Services might break into 'Ladies' and 'Gents' in the hair salon example from earlier. These second-level pages might then break into yet more pages covering each of the individual services on offer, for example:

Services (top-level page) -> Ladies (second-level page) -> Wedding Hair (third-level page)

As well as giving your website visitors a simple and clean way to navigate your website, having an organized structure means that you can optimize each of your third-level pages like crazy to make them really targeted. For example, the page 'Wedding Hair' can be optimized fully for the phrase Wedding Hair, without having to try and work in 'colouring' and 'full head spiral perm' (I had to look that one up) keywords too. Pages so specifically targeted stand a really good chance of showing up on Google.

It also means your website visitors don't have to trawl through a ton of information about something they might have no interest in just to find the content they thought they were clicking through to, leading to a higher chance that they will convert into a buyer.

If you aren't responsible for building your own website, you will want to mention this to the person who is.

Alternatively, you could also think about designing and building your own website. It's actually a lot easier than many people think thanks to the likes of Wordpress and other template-based website creation tools.

Many people assume that they don't have the skills to build their own website, but in my opinion it's worth putting in the small amount of time necessary to learn how to do it yourself – or at least learn to manage it yourself - because of the incredible control and flexibility it gives you, both whilst building the site and then optimizing and updating it later on. For many small businesses, holding on to an out-of-date and poorly optimised website is costing them way more than they might imagine in lost business, and spending some time or money getting it sorted is time and money well invested. Building your own website from scratch needn't be a stressful experience and I have produced a comprehensive video guide showing you how to create your own Wordpress website from scratch, which you can find at www.Get2TheTopOfGoogle.com/offers

Alternatively, feel free to contact me if you would like a well optimised website fully built for you by my company Exposure Ninja.

Niche keywords

If you are competing in a very competitive niche, you might be up against some serious players with a huge amount of online clout, thousands of quality backlinks, subscribers, email lists, busy social media channels and all the rest.

In example might be a local bank, fighting it out with the big multinationals or a local bookstore or London plumber fighting against a vast number of competitors with more established online presences.

If this is the case, then it might not make sense to fight for the most common keywords. If typing in 'plumber' brings up a page of extremely well optimised plumbers and powerful national directory sites, it's going to be a hard-fought battle to come out on top. That's not to say you *can't* or *won't* come out on top, but you'll expend vast amounts of energy winning that war when there might be a more productive use of that time and energy.

Likewise, if you're pushed for time and just want an immediate spike in your results you might also try the strategy I'm about to share.

In virtually all markets, as well as the main keywords, there are more niched keywords. These are searches being performed by fewer people than the more general keyword, but they are more specialized searchers. Depending on the niche, they can also be more valuable customers or be more likely to buy as a result of visiting your site.

Let's look at some examples:

A hair salon fighting a lot of local competition might want to specialize in wedding hair or colouring, and advertise themselves online as the local specialist in this area. This gives them a smaller pool of local competition and allows them to rise to the top faster. So rather than targeting the keyphrase "hair salon" they might choose to target "wedding hair <area>" instead. They'll find it much easier to rank for this 'longer tail' keyphrase, and will generally find it a more efficient use of their time. It's better to be page one for a second level keyword than page 10 for a superstar keyword!

Some people mistakenly think that targeting these niche keywords means that they are surrendering or admitting defeat by choosing to eat from a smaller pie. What they don't realize is that by targeting the more niche keywords, they might actually get *more* work as a result. Not only are there fewer competitors chasing each customer, but also the customers like to feel they are buying from a specialist and therefore the implication is that the product or service will be of greater quality. They will be able to charge higher prices and will find people traveling further to visit 'the specialist'.
So as you can see, choosing to niche in the face of heavy competition from established players can not only make good SEO sense but good business sense.
It's likely that many of the keywords you wrote down will be niche keywords to some extent, and having sized up your competitors you will now be able to decide whether you fancy competing for the big broad strokes keywords or want to develop more towards the niche keywords.
For the most aggressive amongst you, yes, you *can* do both!

Black Hat (Secret, Underground, Illegal) vs White Hat (Clean, Legal) and when to use each one

As well as legitimate ways to make your website show up higher in the rankings (like the ones in this book), there are a number of 'other' strategies which some less scrupulous Search Engine Optimisers use to get websites up the rankings. The advantage of any 'black hat' or improper, devious or spammy techniques is that they can work. Very well. For a time at least.

The disadvantage is that Google doesn't like black hat, and is constantly working to identify and punish websites that use black hat strategies. As time goes on, they get better and better at spotting them, and along with each Google update comes a more aggressive stance against those who try to manipulate search rankings by using spam. Many of the SEOs complaining about Google Penguin penalties are guilty of being lazy or using Black Hat techniques rather than putting the time and effort into using good White Hat human-focussed promotion.

While it can be tempting to peer over to the dark side and think about submitting your website to link farms (websites which can give a lot of low quality backlinks by linking to other websites which link back to them etc), automated spamming software and other ways to get lots and lots of backlinks with no effort, just bear in mind that Google could, and probably will, catch up with you at some point.

And when that point comes, they might choose to punish you by removing you from their listings - that is entirely up to them and you would have no say about it. They have a history of doing it, and they are unafraid to flex their muscles.

Every day I get desperate emails from website owners who have bought low quality links in the past and their sites have disappeared from the Google results page. Their business has suffered and they are desperate, begging for help. It's quite sad to see, so please don't be tempted. If this sounds like you, then keep reading.

As time goes on, the black hat techniques evolve. Currently, it's very easy to buy large numbers of links very cheaply from websites like Fiverr. Some of these links are really low quality link farms, but others appear to offer good value legitimate opportunities to get links that are currently not attracting penalties (they are considered 'Penguin Safe'):

- Manual submissions to social bookmarking websites
- Social media links including:
    - Retweets
    - Posts
    - Pinterest Pins

I don't necessarily discourage use of these, but I would be hesitant about building an SEO strategy *purely* based on these techniques because it's a case of *if* rather than *when* Google catches up with them and lose their effectiveness (or even become damaging to ranking). You can rest assured that some of the smartest minds on the planet are currently processing huge amounts of data with the aim of identifying tell tale signs of social media spamming behavior and fake accounts. By dipping your toe into this water you risk being punished later on.

Hidden Text and Cloaking

Using hidden text and cloaking are two popular 'on page' black hat techniques used by SEOs. They are seen less and less however, as the sites that use them disappear from search results. Nevertheless, they are useful techniques to understand so you can spot them whilst surfing.

Because Google and other search engines look at the text on a website's pages in order to work out what the site is all about, some people will add a huge amount of keyword-rich text to the page in order to give the search engine more 'meat' to chew on. The thinking is that with all that great content, the search engine will reward the website by placing it high in the rankings.

The problem is that a page with this amount of text on can be very off-putting for visitors to the site. So black hat SEOs will hide this text on the page. They might give it the same colour as the background so it's invisible to people reading the site, or they might position it off screen.

The end result is that they can make the page look how they want, whilst also making something that Google sees as content rich.

Another benefit for hiding the content was that you could write it purely for the benefit of search engines, keyword spamming it until it was virtually unreadable (that is having such a high density of keywords that the text doesn't make sense). However, Google wised up to keyword spam and it is now thought that extremely high keyword density is used by Google as a flag that a page is spammy.

So a much better approach is to write good keyword-rich (but not overly so) text that your website visitors actually want to read and find interesting. That way they will stay on your page, might link or share the content and will be more likely to transact with you.

Some black hat SEOs will 'cloak' their pages; that is present a different page depending on whether a human or search engine is looking at the page.

Why? So they can make the page rank highly in Google and then send you to whatever page they want. It might be a similar page or it might be a totally unrelated page. Again, this is similar to the hidden text method in that it means the SEO can show Google a page which is extremely content-rich but send the user to a page which is not burdened with large amounts of text. This technique has been popular for creators of image websites, where text on the page is actually created from images, so there is very little robot readable 'content'. But as people move towards websites with actual text, the need for cloaking for legitimate means has all but disappeared and it's rare that you'll see a website using cloaking appear in the Google results.

White hat overview

So what about white hat techniques? Most SEO companies combine white and grey hat techniques to satisfy their clients' desires for fast results. If you're looking for an SEO company however, I would recommend finding one that sticks strictly to white hat strategies such as building well pages with a good amount of relevant content, making sure the structure of their website is optimized and generating a good number of high quality backlinks.

There's really no reason to stray over to black hat strategies. In the long term, sticking to white hat pays off because any site that is heavily reliant on black hat could be hit hard when Google tweaks its algorithms. And you can rest assured that Google is doing its best to rid its result pages of black hat pages.

The strategies we'll be talking about in the remainder of this book all fall into the category of what is currently considered 'white hat'.

Your Website

Making Google love your website is very important in terms of where it will show up.

We're going to look at a number of different strategies to make your site super-readable by Google and make sure that all your relevant pages are indexed.

But first, some words about different types of websites.

I and many other people who like getting to the top of Google use Wordpress websites. Wordpress is an awesome (and free!) platform which makes it dead easy to build, customize and maintain your website. It's really an absolute gift and if you're starting your website building activities from scratch, I say wholeheartedly USE WORDPRESS! As well as being easy to use, Google really likes Wordpress and finds Wordpress sites very easy to read. This is also very good news.

Many of you will already have your websites set up though, and that's absolutely fine. A well optimized and promoted website will rank highly in Google whether it's built on Wordpress or not.

However, if your website is heavily flash-based - in other words has lots of fancy animation and when you click on different pages the link in the top bar doesn't change, it might be time to consider leaving it behind. Many clients don't like hearing that their flash websites are never going to get to the top of Google but the truth is that Google simply CAN'T read flash. Fewer and fewer people are building with flash and it is becoming obsolete because of the rise of popularity of HTML5, which does a lot of the same stuff and *is* Google-readable.

If you don't mind about Google placement and are ok with people on iPhones and iPads not being able to use your website, then Flash is fine. But its days are numbered and I strongly recommend looking at alternatives.

In fact, I love Wordpress so much I even built a course showing you how to build a Wordpress website from scratch. Check out **www.Get2TheTopOfGoogle.com/offers**
Since publishing this book, I receive a lot of emails from folks who have heard about the joys of Wordpress and are considering moving their website over to Wordpress. There are 3 reasons you might want to do this:

1) You will have greater control over the content on the site and will be able to update it more frequently
2) A lot of the on-page SEO stuff we'll be covering in this book is much easier and quicker if you are using Wordpress.
3) Your site will be more future proof, that is if you want to change the look and feel or layout of your website later on, you can do this relatively simply and you won't have lost all your content or on-page SEO.

If you'd like to know more about moving your site over to Wordpress, I've written a blog post on how/why to do it on the Exposure Ninja website: http:// exposureninja.com/blog

URLs

First, let's look at the URL or address of your website. It's likely that you chose your URL based on who you *are*. Most websites addresses have the company name in them. Obvious, right?
What many people don't think about is that unless people are searching for that company specifically (e.g typing 'Sarah's Hair Salon' into Google), choosing a company name as the domain name might not make as much sense as choosing a more descriptive domain name.
For example, if Sarah's Hair Salon serves customers in Weybridge, one option would be to use a URL like weybridgesalon.com, saloninweybridge.com.

The beauty of domains like this is that they can rank extremely quickly for the phrases they use – for example if someone types 'weybridge salon' into Google, weybridgesalon.com is already at a massive advantage to the other salon websites because the search so closely matches the URL. Now that's not to say that weybridgesalon.com will instantly get to the top of Google for the search 'weybridge salon', but it is likely to get top much faster than a more obscure (from Google's point of view) URL like sarahshair.com.

In all the cases where I have got to the top of Google within a week or so (even in as little as one day in some cases), I have used the main keyphrase as the URL for the website. This is known as using an Exact Match Domain, or EMD.

Using a keyword as your URL is an advantage that's so strong it's extremely difficult to ignore and, given the option, I'll always prefer to build a site with the URL of its desired keywords or phrase. A URL costs hardly anything and can be the cheapest marketing you ever do.

If the client then wants a 'pretty' URL to put on the shop front, van or business cards then I usually buy this name URL as well and point it at the same website using a permanent redirect. That way both sides are happy: the client is happy because they have the URL that looks nice, and the client is happy that they're at the top of Google ☺

If in doubt, go for the descriptive keyword-y URL and then add the pretty URL later.

The place I go to get URLs is currently GoDaddy.com, because they're cheap and once you have an account it's dead easy to buy. But a little tip: never pay full price for domains on GoDaddy.com! There are *always* GoDaddy voucher codes and you'll be able to find the best vouchers available at www.Get2TheTopOfGoogle.com/offers

In September 2012, Google released an update that targets low quality EMDs and there is widespread panic among (spammy black hat) SEOs. Here's the background on this situation:

For years, many website builders have used the 'loophole' of Exact Match Domains to get poor quality websites to rank higher than they ordinarily would. Affiliate websites and simple one-pagers thin on content have been known to rank well despite being the sort of site Google doesn't like to see in its results. This was purely down to the power of exact match domains.

So has this Google update affected the power of Exact Match Domains?

I have a portfolio of about 60 exact match domain websites and I have to say that they have been largely unaffected by the current Google tinkering, so I'm going to stick my neck out and say that Google is not *punishing* exact match domains, but simply remove their super power if they are poor quality content-light websites.

Of course, the websites you and I build are good quality and contain actual content (right?) so we will not be punished for having an EMD and I'm still seeing having an EMD be a distinct advantage, as I have just ranked a site 2nd on Google within 1 week for a competitive geographical keyword using an Exact Match Domain.

Despite this, the most noticeable impact of the EMD update is that having an exact match domain is no longer enough *on its own* to get a site ranking high, quickly. It's still better than not having an EMD, but not as powerful as it used to be.

Multiple Websites

If you already have a well-ranked site for your company name but also want to highly target local traffic as well, you could add a separate website dedicated to targeting this local traffic. With websites so easy to build now there's no reason not to be extremely aggressive in your pursuit of every potential customer online.

I have used this approach in the past, usually with a client that serves 3 distinct areas. I will build a dedicated website for each area and this allows me to really hyper-target the message and keywords used in the site.
The downside of this is that it takes a bit more work and a *lot* more writing - see 'Duplicate Text' later on for the reason you can't just copy and paste the sites changing the area name. Each of these sites can have a geographic exact match domain and link to a location-based Google+ profile (we'll talk more about this later on), and this strategy can be extremely effective for dominating a number of different areas.
It is also an option if you or your client offers a number of different *services*, even if they offer them from the same physical location. One of my clients offers stress management, anxiety treatment and peak performance coaching. To promote each of these distinct services, we have set up smaller 'feeder' or 'satellite' sites targeting one specific category (for example stress management) which then allows us to optimise not just the page, but the entire site (and domain) for this keyphrase and related keyphrases (like 'stress symptoms', 'treatments for stress' etc).
Each of these satellite sites is written individually, linked to a separate G+ profile, submitted and indexed separately - as if they were completely separate sites. As a result, my client has a number of front page results for each of the different services he offers, in addition to his main website which also now ranks very highly.

Structure

We've already had a brief look at structure in the last section where you examined the structure of your competitors' websites, so now it's time to plan your own website's structure and make sure it is fully optimized.
I'm also going to share my own structure guidelines that I use when I build sites for my clients.

Here's an exercise for planning a beautifully optimized website structure.

With a pen and paper draw boxes across the top of the page for each of your website's top-level pages. By 'top-level' pages, remember that we mean pages that are visible when you go to your website's homepage.

So for example, Matt the builder's hypothetical website is at www.mattthebuilder.com.

Matt's top level pages might be:

- Homepage
- Services
- Get a Quote
- Areas Covered
- About Me
- Contact Me

These are all pages that general visitors to Matt's site would be interested in. If you want to find out whether Matt does loft conversions, you would go to 'Services' and from there find loft conversions, so there's no need to have a 'Loft Conversions' page at the top level of his website because this would just clutter up the navigation and confuse his visitors. Think of it a little like a shop window: you don't want to put *every single* product you sell in the shop window but you want people who are looking for something in particular to know where they can find it.

Next we're going to add our second level pages, drawn below our top-level pages and linked with a line. Second-level pages get a bit more specific and start to drill down into the products or services that you offer.

In Matt's case, he offers a general building service as well as loft conversions, and extensions. So from his Services page come three separate pages:

- General Building
- Loft conversions
- Extensions

From his top-level Areas Covered page, come two second-level pages for the two areas that he covers, namely:

- Kent
- East Sussex

The rest of his pages don't have any second-level pages underneath them.

Next, we're going to add any third-level pages. These pages drill down into another level of detail, and can be used to add different angles on the second-level pages. Note that depending on your service, your site might not need third-level pages, but if you are a business that serves a particular location, third-level pages can be a great way to rank for some really juicy keywords.

In Matt's example he has two options.

1) Use his third-level pages underneath 'Services' to target geographical keywords like 'General Building Kent' and 'General Building East Sussex'
2) Go into more detail about the actual services in his third-level pages: 'one storey extensions', 'two storey extensions'.

It wouldn't matter which option he chose really, but I'd probably go for the first option unless you are targeting a real subniche (e.g: Wedding Dresses -> Short Dresses -> Corset Top). So if your clients know what they're looking for and they're hunting something specific, then the more detailed, specialized pages you can offer, the better.

Remember we haven't started to flesh any of these pages out yet, we're simply deciding which pages our website needs.

In Matt the builder's example above, he also had a first-level page called Areas Covered. The reason that any businesses for which location is important should mention the areas they cover plenty of times, is that people tend to type in to Google "builder in <area>".

The second-level pages coming off Matt's Areas Covered page were:

- Kent

- East Sussex

So third-level pages for Kent might include regions in Kent that Matt serves, for example:

- Canterbury
- Maidstone
- Ashford
- Tonbridge

And the same sort of thing for East Sussex – Matt would make a page for each specific area he serves.

This might seem like a pain, and the tempting shortcut is to say, "well Maidstone is in Kent, so saying 'Kent' is enough. I don't need a Maidstone page too."

Well unfortunately, that's not how Google works. When someone searches "extension builder in maidstone", Google is looking for *those* words (as well as a bunch of location indicators that we'll look at later on). Your website needs to give Google those exact words, or variations of them, in order to show up.

Yes, this means building quite a few pages for your website. Rejoice in the effort this takes, because this is the effort that will set you apart from your competitors who don't go to these lengths to dominate Google.

Link Structure

The next important thing to say about website structure is to mention the links that your website uses. If your website uses ugly, code-y links, Google can't read these as well and neither can your website visitors.

What do I mean by ugly code-y links? Links that look like this:
http://mattthebuilder.com/?=314

It's the ?=314 bit at the end that is the ugly bit. Much better is the following:
http://mattthebuilder.com/extensions/one-storey-extensions

Anyone who sees this link can figure out that this page contains information about extensions, in particular one-storey extensions. The same is true for Google.
How your links are set up depends on how your website is built. For some people, there's no (simple) way to change the format of their links. If you have a Wordpress site, it is incredibly easy to change the structure of your links. Simply go into your dashboard, click Settings, choose Permalinks and then the /postname/ option and click save. You are now using what are called 'pretty' permalinks.
It is beyond the scope of this book to go into detail about every possible website platform and how to change link structure but it is worth you spending some time making sure that your permalinks are nice and easy to read for humans and robots alike.

Sitemaps

A sitemap is exactly that - a map of your website.
Because some websites can get pretty complicated in terms of their structure, we can build a map of them and give this map to Google. This allows Google to 'see' all of the pages of the site so we know that they're not missing anything. Now just because Google has a sitemap doesn't mean that *every page of your website will be indexed*, it just mean that every page of your website *can* be indexed, if Google sees fit.
Sitemaps tend to follow the same structure and I'm not going to teach you how to build your own sitemap - again, that is beyond the scope of this book and we're venturing dangerously closely into web design here! But if you're using Wordpress or another content management system there are plenty of plugins that will create your sitemap for you.

Writing for your website

Time to look at fleshing out all those pages you've built/planned.

The key when writing the text for your web pages is to make it human friendly. Remember that there's no point being top of Google if your website visitors are put off by the words on your page sounding all spammy because you've stuffed them so full of keywords.

Having said that, it is extremely important that you write with search engines in mind too. And that means making sure that you use (but not overuse) keywords, put them in titles, use them as links etc.

The first step when you sit down to write for a particular page is to keep in mind the specific keyword or phrase that this page is designed to represent. For Matt the builder, it might be Services -> Extensions -> One-Floor Extensions, so he is going to keep the phrase 'One Floor Extensions' in mind while he writes.

A good starting point is to use this keyword in the title at the top of the page. If you are writing in HTML, put your keywords or phrase in <h1> tags at the top. If you're not getting all code-y, then make your title Heading 1 in the editor.

If you can get away without sounding too spammy, you can then use a variation of your keyword or phrase in an <h2> or Heading 2 underneath this main title.

For example:

<h1>One-Floor Extensions</h1>

<h2>Single storey entensions from the Kent Extension specialist</h2>

Here you have used 'extensions' twice, 'extension' once and a variation of the 'one-floor' phrase, as well as the word 'Kent'. This use of your keyword and variations in the headings shows Google that this page is really highly targeted at that particular phrase and gets you off to a great start on the path to relevance.

If you are a local business, remember to include plenty of mentions of your location in all your website's pages.
How much do you need to write for each page?
Long, boring pages will do you no favours with your visitors but at the same time you need to make sure that you are providing as much information as possible and as many keywords, phrases, variations and modifiers as possible. A good plan of action can be to make a few headings down the page and flesh them out from there. Going back to Matt the builder's example, we might choose to make the following headings for the One-Floor Extensions page:

- One-Floor Extensions
    - General overview talking about one-floor/single-storey (a variation on the keyword) extensions
- One-Floor Extensions in Kent and East Sussex
    - Talking about the areas they build one-floor extensions in, and all the happy customers they have across these regions. Here we are planning to pick up any searches for 'one floor extensions' mentioning the areas we serve.
- Single-storey vs Two-Storey Extensions
    - Another variation on the main keyword, and a comparison that allows lots of legitimate use of the 'one-floor extensions' keyword and its variations
- Types of One-Floor Extensions
    - Allows you to paint pictures in the customer's mind of all the different uses they might have for their new extension. And use that keyword a few more times
- Call the Single-Floor Extension Specialists
    - Yet another key phrase variation as a title on the page. With that I think we are done. You get the picture.

Repeat this process for each and every page. Like anything worthwhile, it does take some effort but just think – competitors probably aren't going to be doing this!

Case Study – How I Pulled Off the Six In Seven First Page Google Results

If you have seen my video about getting to the top of Google, you'll know that one of the things people ask me about a lot is how to show up on the first page of Google multiple times. For one of my clients I was able to make his website show up in top position, and a further 5 times in the next 6 results on page one. So in total, he was 6 of the top 7 results. This sort of Google domination can be extremely valuable for your business and I want to show you exactly how I did it.

The process began with a phone conversation I was having with the client. He came to me as a normal plumber wanting a website, but pretty soon into the conversation he began talking passionately about helping elderly and disabled people stay in their own homes longer by building them walk in showers and baths. The level of service he was offering amazed me; he'd take them out in the car to help them choose the tiles for their bath or shower and he was giving a great product which made a real difference to people's lives.

One problem a lot of plumbers face is that they think their customers know exactly what they do. For example, they assume that just because they install boilers, that if someone needs a boiler installed they know to call the plumber. This is the mistake that many businesses fall prey to by focusing on the *business* or the *product* rather than the *solution* it offers, or better still, the *outcome* for the customer.

The matter is made worse because the people who build plumbers' websites and promote them online don't put in any time to finding out what the plumber's favourite jobs are or what the customers needing these jobs are searching for.

The end result is that there is a big fight for the keyword 'plumber' in every town, and the page is filled with plumbers who all appear completely generic and don't claim to specialize in anything. Having talked to hundreds of plumbers, I can tell you that, so far, every one has a job that they prefer or that they have become known for doing well. Why advertise them as a general plumber when you can make them the specialist in their area for this type of job?

So I asked this plumber from Croydon what he thought of the idea of building a website especially for the walk in baths and showers side of his work. He agreed and I got building.

When it came time to choose a domain name, I wanted something that had real gravity. He was a specialist and I wanted to convey this.

The phrase "walk in baths and showers" is extremely common. I noticed that companies tend to put 'baths' before 'showers'. But the Google Keyword Tool told me that 'walk in showers' was a more common phrase than 'walk in baths'. So I decided to keep the 'walk in showers' phrase intact in my URL and see if I could use walkinshowersandbaths.com.

Bingo! While variations on the regular 'bathsandshowers' phrase were all taken, 'showersandbaths' was all mine. I was in the clear and facing much less competition.

At the end of the day, the customer searches for *either* a walk in shower or a walk in bath. It's unlikely they search for walk in baths *and* showers, so by choosing a variation on the most common phrase I had automatically placed myself outside the most competitive area, whilst giving myself a URL that was actually *more* likely to help me (because the phrase 'walkinshowers' was intact) than the big companies who occupy the rest of this market.

The next step was to add location. The beauty of offering a specialist service in a local area is that you can really hone the entire website to show up for one or two particular phrases. I made sure that the locations my client wanted to target were used in all titles and descriptions and plenty of times in the website text.

By really focusing on those phrases and by choosing to specialize in a pretty narrow niche, you can make something that Google considers far more relevant than all the other competitors in the area who also offer that service, but in addition to the other services they offer.

Once the site was built, it was a case of optimizing the titles and descriptions to include the keywords 'walk in showers', 'Croydon', 'walk in baths', 'elderly', 'disabled' etc.

That is why four of the website's pages rank so highly for the search 'walk in showers Croydon'. The site gets great results for other searches related to this niche too (all results correct as of 21st February 2013):

- 'walk in baths croydon': all 3 top results
- 'elderly baths croydon': all 4 top results
- 'elderly showers croydon': all 3 top results
- 'walk in showers Kingston': all 3 top results
- 'walk in showers sutton': all top 4 results
- 'disabled baths croydon': all top 3 results
- 'disabled showers croydon': top result

As you can see, choosing a highly targeted keyword or phrase and building an entire website around it can produce fantastic results.

So that explains the first four search results for 'walk in showers croydon', but what about the other two?

Those came from high-ranking directories I added the website to. Again, the trick here is to optimize the listing and use the keyword or phrase plenty of times. If your competitors are only using that keyword a couple times on their site and in their directory listings but you build and entire site and create entire directory listings *specifically for* that exact keyword, they don't stand a chance against you. Your content is so highly optimsed for that phrase that Google has no choice but to rank you highly, once it has indexed your pages.

And guess what people in Croydon type when they want a walk in shower installed? It isn't 'general plumber croydon', that's for sure. Be a specialist.

As an update to this section in February 2013, Google sometimes now reduces the number of duplicate results that show up on a single search page. For certain searches like this where previously a number of pages from the site would show up in different positions, Google now sometimes displays a larger result for the website with a list of pages underneath it.

Rather than being a problem, this is fantastic news as it means the listing truly dominates the page. Further, at the time of writing Google is only currently showing 7 organic results on pages that feature one of these 'super listings', so there is 30% less competition on a page we are already dominant on!

Duplicate Text

It can be tempting to copy text between two or more pages. For example, if you have a lot of geographic areas that you serve and you want to write about the identical products and services you offer at each area, it might seem that a nice little shortcut would be to copy all the text and just replace the name of the area. Job done!

Unfortunately, Google doesn't like duplicate text and actually punishes sites which contain a lot of duplicate text, whether it's text copied from other websites or text copied from other pages on the same website.

Just how different the text has to be in order to not be considered duplicate is a hot topic of discussion, but my advice would be to err on the side of caution and actually *write* different text for each page rather than going through changing a few words and reordering the odd sentence here and there. We know that Google generally only gets *tougher* on things it doesn't like rather than more lenient, and it has displayed a dislike for duplicate text so, where possible, avoid it! Genuinely re-written text tends to read better than spun or reordered text anyway, and you might even find yourself explaining more clearly the second or third time around!

If you include pictures on your page, you'll have the option to set alt text – this is the text that shows up if the image doesn't load, or if someone uses software to read the page to them (if they are partially sighted, for example). The jury is out as to how important this alt text is to your Google placement, but I usually put my desired keywords in the alt text anyway just to be sure. Every little helps. But as always, don't get too spammy.

Likewise when uploading pictures to your website, it's good practice to actually name the picture files something relevant to your Search Engine Optimisation. You don't want to get too spammy with this and just use your main keyword over and over again (remember that we're trying to avoid doing anything that looks unnatural), but "Omaha Hair Salon picture.jpg" is a better file name than "IMG00124.jpg".

Stand Out on the Results Page

Obviously showing up highly on Google is just half the battle. Once we're on that results page we then need to make sure the searcher clicks on our website so it's now time to look at some different ways of standing out from your competition.

Meta description

You'll remember the `<meta name="description"`... from our competitor analysis section. You might also remember that this is the text that sometimes shows up in the Google results, so is our chance to 'pitch' our potential website visitors on why they should click on our site rather than the completion. As time goes on, Google has taken to displaying this meta description unedited in the search results less and less. It's now more common for Google to grab a relevant text snippet from the site itself, but even so it is good practice to follow the guidelines for optimising it to attract clicks.

If you aren't the person responsible for building and maintaining your website, it might be tricky to change your meta description, and in fact this section is probably the most technical part of this entire book. It is possible to skip this section and still be OK (although taking care of this stuff does give you a bit of an edge).

How you change your meta description really depends on how your website is built. If you are using Wordpress, it's as simple as installing an SEO plugin like All in One SEO Pack or Wordpress SEO by Yoast (which is currently my favourite). These super-easy plugins allow you to just write in the meta description for each page without getting involved with any code.

As with any of this stuff, if you are unsure how to, for example change meta description in Dreamweaver or another piece of web-building software, a quick Google search should through up some highly relevant results.

So once you know *how* to change your meta description, what should you write?

There are a few things to bear in mind when writing meta descriptions:

1) You want it to be eye catching and trigger interest in potential customers, should they see it. Using boring generic text is never a good idea, so I'll sometimes include the first half of a testimonial in quotation marks so that people will be interested to find out the rest and click on the site. Stating your main benefit or feature that stands you apart from your competition can also work well.
2) Use your keywords by all means, but you really don't need to stuff your meta description full of keywords, it's simply not necessary as the current thinking is that it doesn't have a big effect on your Google ranking. Far more important is to get people to click on your site once they see it.
3) Google will only show 156 characters of your meta description, so make sure that the important stuff is contained in the first 156 characters! There's little point writing a huge long meta description, but used creatively the little '...' s that indicate the description carries on can be a useful source of intrigue for potential website visitors.

An example of a meta description I might use for Sarah's Hair Salon could be something along the lines of:

Sarah's Hair Salon – beautifully cut hair in Weybridge."My hair was so soft and shiny after my visit that my husband just couldn't wait and on the way home he..

At which point Google would chop off the meta description and add the … to signal read on.

How many of Sarah's potential clients *wouldn't* click that website?

It goes without saying that the testimonials you use should always be true, and it's a good idea to include any that you use in the meta description on the page itself to satisfy those who want to find out how the story ended. You then have their attention on your page, and your website can get on with selling your service.

You will have noticed that when you search of a term in Google, any words or variations of those words that appear in the search results are highlighted in **bold**. This is a nice way to get attention as people are now conditioned that the bold writing is more relevant and they are more likely to click on a page that has a higher amount of bold writing in the title and description.

In the Sarah's hair description above, you'll notice that the word 'hair' is used 3 times, 'salon' is used, and 'weybridge' also. The name 'Sarah's Hair Salon' is also in there as it's possible that people will be searching for Sarah's Hair Salon in particular. All of these words would be brought out in **bold**.

Meta titles

So that's the meta description taken care of, and now let's look at one of the most important parts of your website's appearance on the Search Engine Results Page, your meta title. This is the title of the website that appears in the Google results.

Just like the meta description, this title is limited by Google and anything over 70 characters will be chopped off.

And also just like meta description you want to include your keywords and you can afford to be slightly more generous with their use here as people generally skim the titles and the ones with most bold highlighted text tend to cause the reader to pause and check out the meta description. People are also far more used to seeing 'keyword stuffed' titles than meta descriptions.

It's a good idea to use your keyword early on in your meta title - like, right at the start. Sarah's meta title could be, for example:
Weybridge Hair Salon - Sarah's Hair Salon | Free Hair Consultations
Again, the first 3 words would be **bold**, as would words 4,5 and 7. That's a lot of bold text, but the title is still informative, enticing and would probably beat other generic titles on the page thanks to the mention of free consultations.
The process for changing your meta title is going to be the same as changing your meta description, and again is beyond the scope of this book to list every possible way in each different website building application, but if in doubt a Google search should show you the way.

Meta Keywords

Many times, if you see a box allowing you to insert meta description and meta title text for your webpage, you will also see a box for you to input 'meta keywords'. It is a nice idea that just by typing in the keywords we want to rank for Google will make us show up, but in reality Google ignores the meta keywords tag because it is so easy to manipulate. In the olden days of the internet they held more weight, but nowadays their biggest function is showing smart SEOers from your competition which keywords you have considered important and would like to rank for, saving them the time it takes to do the research for themselves.
I don't tend to use meta keywords at all.

Rich Snippets: How to Make People Click On Your Website Even If It's Underneath Your Competitors

The beauty of having good meta descriptions and meta titles is that they can give your webpage more visitors because they catch people's eyes - even if they are below your competitors on the results page. There is another nice little trick I have been using lately to make my clients' websites stand out on the results page.

You might have seen whilst using Google that some bigger directory websites now have review stars next to their listings. They do this to stand out from the crowd and, from my own tests, it works.

I'm going to show you how to add these stars to your website's Google result.

hreviews

Rich snippets are a name given to special text on a webpage that is accepted by Google to be information about a product or service and formatted in an agreed way. Examples of uses for rich snippets are: business cards (so you can let Google know that your website is linked with a particular business), product details (this is why you sometimes see particular Amazon products show up in the listings, for example) and reviews (which is where the stars come from). There are many others as well, but we are going to be concentrating on the reviews for now.

It's actually very straightforward to add reviews to your website, particularly if you are using Wordpress or another content management system. If you are not, then it is still quite easy to add them in the first place, but integrating a system that allows your customers or readers to continually rate your website is a little more tricky.

What you have to remember is that people can get into trouble for adding fake reviews or reviews of themselves so it's always a good idea to have a hard copy of any reviews your customers make so that you could back yourself up, should your reviews' legitimacy ever come into question.

Anyway, with that out of the way let's look at how to add hreviews (what we call these review rich snippets) to your website.

If you're using Wordpress, simply go and download the free plugin Customer Reviews. This plugin allows you to include a button on each page of your website that your customers can click to add their review of your business, product or service. It's really that simple.

If you're using plain html, when you add a review or testimonial to your website, turning this into an hreview is simply a case of adding a bit more code.

This example is taken from the microformats.org website and shows a restaurant hreview:

```
<div class="hreview">
<span><span class="rating">5</span> out of 5
stars</span>
<h4 class="summary">Crepes on Cole is awesome</h4>
<span class="reviewer vcard">Reviewer: <span
class="fn">Tantek</span> -   <abbr class="dtreviewed"
title="20050418T2300-0700">April 18, 2005</abbr></span>
<div class="description item vcard"><p>
<span class="fn org">Crepes on Cole</span> is one of
the best little   creperies in <span class="adr"><span
class="locality">San Francisco</span></span>. Excellent
food and service. Plenty of tables in a variety of
sizes for parties large and small.  Window seating
makes for excellent people watching to/from the N-Judah
which stops right outside. I've had many fun social
gatherings here, as well as gotten plenty of work done
thanks to neighborhood WiFi.</p></div>  <p>Visit date:
<span>April 2005</span></p>
<p>Food eaten: <span>Florentine crepe</span></p> </div>
```

If the sight of the above puts you off ever eating food again, then simply ask your web guy or gal to make sure your testimonials are hreviews. If they refuse or threaten to charge you lots of money, fire them, download Wordpress and install the Customer Reviews plugin instead.

You need to be able to control your website, and Wordpress is just so easy to use. See my Wordpress Course for a step-by-step guide to building a Wordpress website from scratch in less than an hour.

If you look closely at the code about, you'll see that we have a number of different categories. In the first line you'll see `hreview`, which simply tells Google's robots that this is, in fact, an hreview.

In the next line we have the rating out of 5 stars. This rating is what shows up in the Google results. After that we have a short summary of the review, followed by the reviewer's name, then the date of the visit.

Then you have the description of the item, and included in this is the organization's name ("`fn org`") and location.

Not all of this info is necessary, and I personally only include the following fields in my clients' reviews:

- Name of reviewer: (customer in <area> if I don't know their name)
- Date of service/visit/purchase
- Rating (out of 5 stars)
- Review

Aggregate Reviews vs Recent Reviews

Google displays your review stars in a couple different ways according to how you have your webpage set up:

If you have a page with loads of reviews from different people on, then what Google will do is take an average number of stars from each review and show this average on the results page, along with some text like "from 6 reviews" or how many reviews you have on that page.

If you only have one review on that page however, Google will just show that review along with the name of the reviewer.

Both methods are useful, and for some businesses I actually *prefer* to only have one review on most pages and I'll explain why:

Let's say that your website's homepage target keywords are 'electrician in Edinburgh'. You obviously also want to get some stars showing up with your homepage, but you probably don't want to devote half your homepage to all your most recent reviews, so what you can do instead is just include one review. Then instead of using the reviewer's name, you can use 'Customer in Edinburgh' (if they're actually from Edinburgh, of course).

That way, when someone searches 'electrician in Edinburgh' and sees your homepage in the results page, they will see the stars from your reviewer, plus the text "Reviewer in Edinburgh". MAJOR relevance here! Do you think that searcher is going to click on your site? Of course!

Google+ Integration

Authorship Markup

If you've noticed that some websites have a picture of the writer's face next to them in the Google results, then you've seen authorship markup in action. We're going to go through the process now to get your or your client's website showing up with your (or their) picture.

The benefit of having your picture next to your page in the search results is that it draws the eye of the searcher and attracts more clicks. The most recent stats I saw claimed that results with a picture of the author next to them improved their click through rate (the percentage of people that click on them) by 100% - they *doubled* their CTR. This is big news not just because it means they attract more website visitors, but also because if Google is looking for signals as to which pages searchers find useful, and here's a page that is getting a ton of clicks - guess what? They're going to take that into consideration when deciding whom to rank where.

So as you can see, even though using authorship markup won't lead directly to better rankings, it's likely to lead to better rankings over time by increasing click through rate.

So how do we implement authorship markup on our websites?

To get started, you need to be a part of Google+, Google's attempt at social networking. Whatever you think of it I encourage you to get signed up and start using it, if only for the SEO benefits!

You can sign up by signing into Google and clicking the You+ link at the top left hand corner of the Google page. This will guide you through the steps to create your profile (if you haven't already) and add a headshot photo. This photo is very important as it will be the one we will get showing up next to your website result in the search pages, and Google will only show it if it's a good quality headshot.

It's best to fill out your profile as completely as possible to make it more appealing to people that end up there as a result of seeing you in the search results.

Once your profile is up-to-date and looking good, you need to go back and click 'Edit Profile' and go to the section marked "Contributor To". In this section, you can list the websites that you contribute content to. Of course, you'll want to list your main website here. This is the first part of integrating authorship markup.

Once that is done, it's time to put the relevant code on your website to link *back* to your Google+ profile and confirm that indeed this person *is* a contributor to this website. A two-way link between your website and Google+ profile gives Google the reassurance that you are indeed the author of the content.

Somewhere on the page that you want to appear in the search results (normally your homepage), add the code: <a href="[profile_url]?rel=author">Google</a>

Replace [profile_url] with your Google+ profile URL, like this:, <a href="https://plus.google.com/109412257237874861202?rel=author">Google</a>

Your link must contain the ?rel=author parameter because if it's missing, Google won't be able to associate your content with your Google+ profile.

For many of my clients, I put this authorship link in the footer of the website because I want their Google+ profile linked to every page on the site.

Google+ Local Integration

If your website is for a local business, I would recommend linking it to a Google+ Local page. The techniques involved here are covered in more detail by my book 'How to Get to the Top of Google Places/Google+ Local'.

Google+ Local is Google's new version of Places, with added social networking extra juicy features. Because +Local is still relatively new, things are changing all the time but some of the benefits are:

- The inclusion of big, eye catching address blocks for certain Google+ Local associated websites
- A presence on the Google map
- If the searcher is signed in to Google+ and their friends like your page, this will show in the search results and make your page more likely to show up (this is Google's 'Search Plus Your World' – their attempt to make personalized and more relevant search results for Google+ users).

To link your website to a Google+ Local page, first you need to create the page. If you are already signed up to Google+, then you can choose More -> Pages then click to create a page for a local business. Go through the process of setting up your page, adding as much information, pictures and videos as you can. On the main profile section you will see somewhere to fill in the address of your website. Once you have done this, you'll see a button to 'link website'. Clicking this gives you a block of code to include on your website.

Again, I usually put this in the footer or towards the bottom of the homepage. Where you put it is up to you and depends on how many people you expect to interact with your Google+ page.

Once you have added the code to your page, head back over to your Google+ page and click the button to confirm the code is on your site. You'll get a message from Google saying that they need to carry out more tests to confirm the link, and you're done!

Now you play the Google+ waiting game as you wait to find out when and how much of this new Google+ information will show up in the search results. Most of the time, authorship markup shows up fairly quickly - usually within a couple of weeks. Address and map location can take a lot longer.

Other Website Considerations

It's important that your website is structurally solid and there are no holes. By that I mean that there are no broken links, pages that don't exist or any of the sort of thing that a critical Google robot might look at and think 'hmm, this website isn't good quality'. One good way to do this is through Google Webmaster tools, which we'll be looking at in more detail shortly, but it's also a good idea to check every link and button on each page to check they're all taking you to the right place and you're not getting any errors or 404 pages.

Promoting Your Website Elsewhere

Once you have your website set up and fully readable by Google, it's time to get promoting it online. Promotion is an incredibly important part of getting your website to show up top of Google, and Google really likes websites that have lots of good quality links pointing at them.

We talked a bit about PageRank earlier in the book and how PageRank 'flows' to the sites that are linked from that web page.

So the ideal scenario is that you get lots of juicy links from websites that have high PageRank and are talking about a relevant topic.

How to Show Up On The First Page Of Google Using Other People's Websites

The quickest and easiest source of links for many businesses is directory websites. There are a whole host of free and paid options out there, and the best choices for you depend on your market and type of business (whether you are purely online, offline or a combination).

Having your website listed in lots of directories is useful for three reasons:

1) The links from the directories back to your website might push your website up the Google rankings
2) If the directories are high quality and loved by Google (these are the best sort) and your entries are well optimized, then these entries themselves might start ranking high on Google. This is the case with Yelp.com, for example, which is currently a bit of a Google darling.
3) Potential customers who somehow end up on the directory website might find your listing and give you a call. However, don't let the directory website blurb fool you – according to my extensive research and experience

with dozens of clients and their directory listings, this is incredibly uncommon.

You'll notice that most free directory websites offer a paid membership, which usually involves promise of more exposure and being listed at the top of searches for your category. If you really want to test this, feel free. But primarily we are using the directories for their Google juice and not the traffic that is already using the directory website, in which case a free listing is adequate.

Whatever business you are in, there are some ways to maximize your Google ranking with your listings:

- Be sure to use your business name in the title, but also the main keyword you are targeting. For example "Matt The Builder – Extension building specialist serving Kent and East Sussex"
- In the description, be sure to use your keywords plenty of times, but make the description readable for humans too – you never know, this listing might rank above your own website for a while so think about what your potential customers would want to read in order to get in contact with you
- If the directory allows it, add links to your website in the description and use your main keyword as anchor text (for example your link might look like this: <a href="http://mattthebuilder.com">Extensions Builder in Kent</a>, and would show up on the page as Extensions Builder Kent. While most directories automatically add nofollow to your links (meaning that you don't get Pagerank from the link), they don't *all* add nofollow so if in doubt, add a link.
- Make sure your contact details are *exactly* the same as any contact details you use in your Google Places listing and on your website, if relevant. For more information about Google Places, how to claim your listing and optimize it, see my Guide to Google Places.
- If the directory gives you the option to add pictures and/or videos, opening hours, payment options etc, add

these. Every directory wants its listings to look fully kitted-out and many will reward listings that have been filled out completely with higher ranking. It also converts more visitors and makes you stand out from the dozens/hundreds/thousands of other generic listings that will likely make up the bulk of the directory

Market-specific directories vs General directories

Whatever business you are in, and whether it's primarily offline or online, there will usually be online directories that are targeted specifically for you. Likewise, if you are a local business serving customers in one particular area you will find that there are local directories for listing all businesses in that area.

In general, these highly targeted directories are a very good idea. We've seen that particularly post-Penguin Google gives importance to links from websites that are targeted and relevant. It's also more likely that visitors to that directory will be potential customers for you as they have already narrowed themselves down either geographically or by interest to be on the site in the first place.

The best method I know for finding new directories to add mine and my clients' websites to, is to Google each of my keywords and look for directory listings in the results. When I find a directory page, I'll add it to my list of directories to submit to.

While using the Backlink Finder tool mentioned earlier you might also notice that your high-ranking competitors are listed in certain directories and these will make good additions to your directory list.

Adding Too Many Listings At Once

There has been plenty of talk online of Google 'punishing' websites who seem to get unnatural numbers of links all in a short period of time. The reasoning is that this appears like spammy behavior, or an obvious attempt at manipulating Google's rankings. While the argument about the logic behind this theory is something completely separate, it's somewhat irrelevant to our plan. The beauty of most of the directories you will find is that your entry requires some sort of manual approval.

This approval can take minutes, hours, days, weeks or even months. So adding your website to 50 directories over the course of a day won't create 50 directory profiles instantly, but your exposure will be more spread out over time. Even if adding your site to 50 directories in a day did create 50 profiles instantly, Google would take some time to crawl these directories and add your listing to its index, so there's really no need to worry about it.

Manual Listing vs Automatic Listing

As with any repetitive online task, it can be tempting to wonder about a software solution to get all these directory listings taken care of.

The advantages of doing it manually is that you get a greater level of acceptance. Directories tend to favour manual submission and many will reject automatic submission instantly, and might even ban you from submitting again.

Then there is accuracy. Obviously when you are in charge of adding your listing, you are going to be in the right category and with all your details in the right place.

Automatic submission doesn't offer this level of accuracy but it does offer significant timesaving if you are responsible for submitting lots of different sites to a number of directories. If you are just optimizing the one website, then even setting up the submission could take a long though.

I personally use manual submission all the time, and if I'm going to outsource directory submission I will make sure that the outsourcer is doing it manually rather than automatically.

Outsourcing Directory Listing

There are plenty of services out there offering directory submission. While some services can seem extremely cheap, and therefore attractive, they will often use automatic submission, exactly the same description each time (and could therefore be flagged by Google as duplicate content) and submit to poor quality directories (which could even harm your Google rank).

Also remember that with any directory submission service, the advertised number of submissions will tend to be far higher than the number of listings you will actually receive, as many directories will reject the submitted listing for whatever reason.

Article Submission

Another way of getting more exposure for your website online is to write and submit articles about a relevant topic, with links to your website in. The advantage of this approach is that you can often get an article on websites that you wouldn't be able to get just a link on.

For example, if you're writing a How To article, then there are plenty of websites like ehow.com and wikihow.com that feature how to articles. Google likes these websites because they generally have high quality information and aren't too spammy. Be warned though that high quality sites like these are high quality for a reason - submissions are scrutinized and it can be tricky to get your article published. What's more, the rules tend to be pretty tight about linking, which can be a real bummer if the whole purpose of the article writing exercise is to generate good quality backlinks! But whether or not they contain links, published articles position you as an expert, and put your name in front of a large number of people on the web who are interested in your field.

Like directory sites, there are a huge number of very poor quality article submission sites that allow any article to be submitted no matter what the topic or if it even makes sense. A quick browse of some of the submitted 'articles' can reveal a large number of keyword stuffed, unreadable gobbledygook. These low quality sites are best avoided as they will more than likely be flagged as spam by Google, so any links appearing on them could do you more harm than good.

One of the best places to get articles submitted is, believe it or not, your local newspaper's website. They are often pretty desperate for content and a quick article on helping your town's residents decide what hair cut to get, hot new property trends in 2013, fashionable uses for single-storey extensions etc can be something of real interest to local people. These sites are also more likely to allow you to link to your website and again provide targeted traffic which can lead to real business.

Often an email or phone call to the news desk editor will be sufficient to get your article online.
Many website owners struggle with a subject for their article, but a quick browse of local newspaper story subjects should put your mind at ease: often there ain't a whole lot going on to write about! A story about the new website being unveiled may or may not be of sufficient interest to their readers to get a decent sized article in, but a story about a reader-exclusive offer might. Stories about celebrities or quasi-celebrities make good subject matter, and if you have any interaction with anybody who is even slightly famous during the running of your business, be sure to grab a picture with them or get a testimonial as the power this has is immense.

Duplicate Content

We talked about Google's stance on duplicate content (it doesn't like it) at various points in this book, and unsurprisingly duplicate content in submitted articles or directories is another no-no (with the exception of listings of your name, address and phone number which should always be precisely duplicated).

One of the most common ways grey or black hat SEOs use to create duplicate content online is to use article 'spinners'. Spinners change the content of articles while aiming to keep the overall message the same. For example changing "Sarah's Salon has been trading to local customers in Weybridge since 2011" to "Sarah's Salon has been selling to nearby clients in Weybridge since 2011".

The content of the sentences is nearly identical, and the level of spinning is adjustable allowing thousands of different variations of each sentence. While this can seem appealing to try and get past Google's tough stance on duplicate content, my position is this:

Google knows about spinning. Websites with spun content tend to be full of spam. Google is constantly working to rid its search results of websites full of spam. Therefore, even if you can get away with spun content now, it's unlikely that this shortcut will remain for much longer.

Again, the alternative is more time consuming and laborious but produces far better results, and that is to manually rewrite the content. This means manual rewriting of directory descriptions and any articles you submit. It takes time, but means that you can be sure your entries won't get flagged for duplicate content and also that any potential customers who stumble across your entry won't be put off by a spammy vibe (you can *always* tell spun content - you might have seen blog comments that have been spun so far they make absolutely no sense whatsoever).

Currently, nobody in the outside world knows for sure how Google measures duplicate content and what level of similarity triggers alarm bells, but what you can be sure of is this: their detection process for duplicate content will get better and better over time and you can bet your bottom dollar that there are some very clever people working on precisely this, *right now*. So in my opinion the best approach is to avoid spinners and automatic submission wherever possible.

Linkbuilding 2.0

In order to boost the Pagerank of your website, it helps to have a number of links pointing at it. Directory websites and links from customers/suppliers/industry association websites are great, but if you are going to build lots of links then it might be time to consider embarking on a link building campaign.

The problem with link building is that a lot of it looks spammy, and in the past almost all link building has been very low quality: things like spamming blog comments and spinning articles with a link at the end. Every couple weeks a new piece of magical SEO software is released that allows the user to find and get 10,000 new links to their site, completely free, using the latest underground secret Russian strategy or whatever.

The truth is that this stuff *can* still work and get some good results - for now. But I don't advise it at all. Google is working hard to clamp down on this junk promotion and its days are numbered. With every new Google update I brace myself for the latest stream of emails from desperate website owners whose sites have vanished because they embarked on a new whizz bang link 'scheme', and I really don't want you to be among them.

But links are still important, so what is the solution?

Over the past year or so, I've been working with my ninjas to develop linkbuilding 2.0.

Sounds exciting, no?

No.

But it is pretty cool when it gets sites ranked high!

The lines are blurring between SEO and general promotion online. Linkbuilding 2.0 is about promoting the site online, with SEO included. In this way it mimics the organic appearance of online popularity, which is really what Google is trying to measure by analyzing backlinks. It also has the potential to drive real potential customers to a site because the links are showing up in places that they are hanging out already.

Linkbuilding 2.0 uses 3 different strategies:

1) Forum posting – This is not the old school spamming!
2) Blogging
3) Quality article writing and submission

I cover point 3 elsewhere in this book, so for now we'll focus on the first 2 strategies.

Forum Posting

Gone are the days when you could sign up to any old forum and start spamming links to your site. Not only does that no longer give you any useful link juice, you're fairly likely to get banned by a moderator. What is much better is the linkbuilding 2.0 strategy of engaging in the forum discussions. By asking questions, giving advice and responding to people talking about things relevant to your business and market in forums dedicated to these subjects, you are positioning yourself right in front of your target customers. If you include a link in your forum signature to your site, every post you make will create a new backlink to your site. These links are high quality because the content of the forum is *relevant* to your site, and you are becoming an authority in the eyes of the other forum users.

Yes, this is more time consuming than paying for 10,000 forum backlinks on Fiverr, but guess what? It's also better for your business.

Whenever we are embarking on a linkbuilding 2.0 campaign for a client, we'll set up forum profiles on a number of the highest ranking and most authoritative public forums in their industry, then watch the conversations. If something comes up that is relevant, we will join the conversation and try to add as much value as possible.

Let's look at an example:

Say that our site is for a hair salon who has decided to target wedding hair because it is high ticket and the stylists enjoy doing it. We would find the most suitable wedding ideas, hair style and women's forums and make profiles on them, often using the identity of the website owner (with their permission of course!). We'd then go into the forums and look to add to the discussion wherever someone was talking about wedding hair or wedding ideas. We would post pictures from the site if relevant, and include a link to the wedding hair pages on the site in our forum signature and generally try engage with the people and ask questions.

Blogging

The next strategy is all about blogging. Guest blogging is where you get an existing blog to run some of your content, and this is a great option if there are blogs in your industry that are open to publishing guest posts. The secret to getting your posts published is to make them good quality and valuable to the readers - remember that the blog owner isn't going to post just any old junk promoting a site they've never heard of, so if you can find a way to create something really interesting or useful (a survey, opinion piece or article about the trends in your industry are good starting points) then you are much more likely to get some traction getting your article published.

Note that you don't have to be too over the top in promoting your site here. As long as there is a link in the "about the author" section, that should suffice. Of course if it's relevant to add a link or two in the article then you should do that, but don't compromise the feeling of quality or legitimacy.

If there aren't any blogs in your industry that would be happy to run a guest post, then you're going to have to start your own. This can be far less effort than it sounds, and setting up an account on blogger or tumblr is a good place to start. You'll want to create a blog that covers a topic relevant to your website, but that doesn't look purely like a platform to promote your services. An example for the hair salon owner's blog could be "wedding hair ideas", or the broader "wedding style".

You can link to your website from your author bio or "about me" page, as well as in the posts themselves, but also remember to link to other websites from around the net. As a rule, it shouldn't be too obvious that this blog is here only to position you and get some good links coming in to your website, but it should actually be interesting and valuable to your target customers as well.

I know that for many website owners, these linkbuilding 2.0 strategies will prove too time consuming to carry out themselves, and that is perfectly understandable in which case you might be wise to outsource it. Clearly the requirements in a linkbuilding 2.0 link builder are more advanced than a regular link builder as they are required to create the illusion of expertise (or at the very least, interest) in the market they are promoting. At Exposure Ninja we have some experienced workers in this field, and our linking ninjas always spend time researching and understanding the market before heading into forums and blogs to present their expertise. If you would like to discuss a linkbuilding 2.0 campaign, please get in touch through the website or email me tim@exposureninja.com

Be Careful of Spammy Sites

In Google's Panda Update, one of the key talking points was the punishment of low quality sites designed purely to trick visitors into viewing them and get high rankings in Google. The sort of sites that have been affected are those annoying sites that show up looking really relevant until you click on them to find huge amounts of seemingly random text, links and general gibberish.

What's more, Google is now not only punishing these sites, but also punishing sites that these sites *link to.* Recently Google Webmaster tools began warning webmasters when a number of low quality websites were linking to them, and suggesting that they go through and get these links removed. This is a real pain in the ass if you have thousands of links from crappy websites.

What this means is that many websites that relied on lots of low quality backlinks from these spam sites started plummeting down the rankings.

Many website promoters were forced to change their strategy literally overnight in order to get their websites back up in the rankings, and the fallout has been huge.

Google has declared war on spammy sites that frustrate its users, and for that reason you should always check that any sites you are about to list your website on are clean and non-spammy. Otherwise you could find your site blacklisted by Google for appearing on many of these low quality sites. This is another reason to avoid automatic submission or outsourcing to less than scrupulous companies who have no regard for the quality of sites that they submit their clients addresses to, as you have little assurance that you won't end up being associated with one of these spam hangouts.

Social Media

Social media has taken the world by storm, and the possibilities of Twitter, Facebook, Foursquare and the like can seem to be endless.

Google likes social media too and joined the party with its Google+ social network, and while it's still relatively early days, we're beginning to see how its integration might affect search habits and results. Early on Google gave what many considered to be an 'unfair advantage' to Google+ results in the search pages, causing considerable outcry from the tech world. Google responded by actually *punishing itself* and Google+ results in the search results as their way of saying sorry. It's currently too early to tell how Google+ will affect the world of advertising in the long-term, but as we've seen there are already some interesting innovations such as authorship markup and Google+ Local that can have an effect on our world.

We do know that Google uses social media presence as a sign of life for businesses and websites. It indicates activity, popularity and new content and this is all good news in terms of your Google ranking.

What many companies do is set up a Facebook and Twitter profile, and link these to their websites. Then what commonly happens is that these Facebook and Twitter profiles never get used. As an SEO recommendation they seemed like a good idea at the time, but in reality the business owner ends up being the one responsible for updating their profile and the important tasks involved in running the business inevitably get in the way.

Whether you choose to use social media should depend on the following criteria:

- Whether your competitors use it. If they do and are active, then it's a good idea for you to join them in the world of status updates and tweeting. In all likelihood, they wouldn't be doing it if it wasn't paying or creating some sort of return.

- Whether or not your customers use it, and whether they will value interacting with you. For example, almost everyone uses washing detergent, but how many want hourly tweets about washing detergent from the manufacturer clogging up their timelines? On the other hand, the local plumber who regularly posts money saving tips, new trends in bathroom design, boiler maintenance tips and special seasonal discounts etc might be extremely interesting to, say, landlords who use social media, and these folks are likely to be very valuable customers.
- Whether you will actually *use* it. If you know straight away that you won't, there's little point bothering. There's nothing that's more of a turnoff than out of date content and unused social media profiles.
- Whether you are *already* being talked about on social media. Some companies need to check Twitter more often. People have no hesitation about complaining over social media, and if they receive a substandard service their followers could be hearing about it for a long time to come. If your company becomes infamous on twitter, the best course of action is to get on there and try to rectify the situation rather than ignore it.

Many larger corporations understand the importance of negative word of mouth and have dedicated teams of people on twitter finding and solving customer problems when they happen, and before the dissatisfaction can spread or get worse. I distinctly remember back in 2009 complaining about the service I was getting from a certain British telecoms company. While I was trying to navigate my way through seemingly endless automated menu options to speak to someone extremely unhelpful in India or another popular call centre destination, I tweeted my fury. To my utter shock and amazement, I got a reply from their official account asking for my customer details so they could get the problem fixed. I replied and within minutes they had tracked down the source of our slow line. Meanwhile, I was still on hold on the phone.

If your website covers a market that people are really passionate about (fashion, food, motorbikes, cameras or photography, for example) it's a good idea to force yourself to use social media whether or not any of your competitors use it. There is an unbelievable hunger out there for up-to-date information about subjects for which people are passionate, and if you can position yourself as an expert in your category with some interesting, insightful and informative tweets or status updates, you will generate quite a following and this can be a huge asset in terms of sales and visits to your site.

Using Videos to Leapfrog Pages and Pages of Your Competitors

Google will often include videos in its search results, and unless you're in a market where lots of your competitors use video, it's unlikely that they will be using this tactic to try and show up on the first page of Google. Showing up with a video can be a great way to leapfrog onto the front page very quickly, and if you are the only video on the front page you will stand out. The beautiful thing is that your website doesn't have to be *anywhere near* the front page of Google for your video to get to the front page.

Lots of people automatically disregard making videos because they think they'll be really expensive, time consuming and they don't really know where to start.

Rather than being big expensive productions, there are plenty of companies who provide short promotional video tools online and within a couple minutes you can have a promotional video for your website. Head over to www.Get2TheTopOfGoogle.com/offers for my recommendations.

When you are making your video, be sure to title it with your keywords. Once it's finished, download it and then upload it to as many video websites as you can find, giving it the title of your main keywords. Then in the description, add some keyword-rich words about your website and a link (if possible using your keywords as the anchor text).

The best video websites I have seen for getting videos on the front page are:

- Dailymotion
- Viddler
- Metacafe
- Youtube

If these are well-optimised listings (with good titles and descriptions), you can sometimes get multiple instances of the same video showing up on the front page. I currently have 3 videos in the top 4 Google results for one of my clients, with the same video on YouTube, Daily Motion and Metacafe. The main website is ranking on the first page as well, but it's the videos that grab people's attention!

Of course, you'll also want to embed the video on your website because not only will it catch the eye of your website visitors, but Google likes videos and, in particular, videos with the same titles as your keywords and it further establishes the relevance of your website for your chosen keywords.

Some people have been using videos to sell their products and services online for years, but for some reason most websites haven't really ventured into the world of video. You can take advantage of this and use it to stand out from your competitors.

Your Strategy

How to Plan An Unstoppable Google Strategy

So now you have the tools at your disposal to plan and implement a killer SEO. In this section I will help you sketch out your SEO plan, fill in the gaps and then get to work implementing it.

Initial Research

The initial research is absolutely key. In order to beat your competition you need to know their strengths, weaknesses and where to exploit them. You also need as good an understanding as anyone about your market's habits online. The first step is doing the basic research: searching for your product or service and seeing what comes up. Making a note of your competitors, who is showing up and what they are showing up with (titles and descriptions in the Google results). Seeing how the results change if you search for a variation on your main term – is it the same few websites at the top of Google for each variation and different product or service category or are they all dominated by one or more players?

Next you'll be studying their websites and noticing the following:

- Which keywords do they seem to be targeting, and how often do they use them on the page?
- How much text is on their pages?

- What are the pages called?
- Do they use different pages for each product or service, or is everything on one big page?
- How is the website structured?
    - Are there a lot of pages all linked from the homepage, or do you go through different levels of pages to find more and more specialized content?
- Are they using social media?
- What do their meta description, meta title tags and meta keywords say? (find these by right clicking on an empty area of the page and clicking 'View Source')
- How big is the site?
    - Are there a lot of pages?

Remember that the goal at this stage is just to absorb what the competition are doing and make a note of anything that particularly stands out, surprises you or that is significantly different to your website. You'll also want to jot down any keywords that you hadn't thought of.

Keyword research (keyword tool)

The next step is to think about keywords. These are the terms that your potential website visitors will be searching in order to find your site. To begin with, make a note of every possible way of describing what you do or sell, and variations of these descriptions. Remember that people online search in a particular way: rather than searching for "Architect based in Bristol", they'll write "architect Bristol" or "Bristol architect".

Next, we're going to expand our keyword research by heading over to the Google Keyword tool. To get the tool, simply Google "Keyword Tool" and click the link.

Google's keyword tool allows us to do research into exactly what people are searching for, and related searches.

To begin with, put in your main keywords and choose your region. Google will show you the average number of searches for your terms each month, and how many of these searches are local in nature.

The Keyword Tool also gives you an indication of the level of competition for paid adverts for that term. While this doesn't necessarily indicate the level of competition for getting top spot of the *organic* Google listings, it can be a useful indication of the commercial intent of the typical searches for that term. If people are willing to pay to appear on the page, it's usually to profit so you can be fairly sure that this keyword search tends to result in purchases.

In the box below the list of the keywords you enters, you'll also see a list of Google's suggestions for similar searches, and this can be an extremely useful insight into the searching habits of your customers.

For example, using the Google Keyword Tool to search for searches similar to 'plumber' shows that there is also a large volume of searches for 'plummer'. This information is interesting and suggests that it might be worth including a few references to this misspelling on your website.

Remember to also note down any modifiers: words that can be added to your keyword or phrase that your potential customers might be searching for. For example "emergency", "24-hour", "local", "trusted". By adding these modifiers to keywords on your page you can often pick up the 'low hanging fruit' and get good placement for particular phrases that your competitors might be ignoring.

Once you have your list of keywords, pick the 5 main ones you will be targeting. These might not necessarily be the most popular ones according to the Keyword Tool, but will certainly be relevant to your product or service and website content.

Building pages & Content

The next stage of your plan is to sketch out your website's structure, whether or not you plan to change it. If you don't have control over your own website and it is not currently ranking well on Google, this is the best time to decide to go it alone and take responsibility for building your own site - or at least having a site built that you can get into and make necessary changes. It can be far quicker to start from scratch than negotiate with web designers who don't understand SEO (not to mention the cost savings of doing it yourself) and the bottom line is that no one will do a better job of promoting you than you.

Wordpress is extremely easy to use for beginners and once it is set up it's extremely easy to get in and make changes. See Get2TheTopOfGoogle.com/wordpress for information about my easy-to-follow guide to setting up your own Wordpress website in less than an hour.

When sketching out your website structure, you will want to decide on your top level pages (Home, Products/Services, About, Contact) and then any second level pages will need to branch off these top level pages. These second level pages should be built with general keywords in mind (e.g. Ladies Hair, Gents Hair; Wedding Dresses, Ball Gowns; Sports Cars, Saloons). Then decide on third level pages that might branch off these second level pages. These third level pages should be targeted at specific keywords or phrases (Popular ladies hairstyles, smart ladies hairstyles; Corset top wedding dresses, Satin wedding dresses; Cabriolets, 2-Seaters).

The aim is to have your website structure neatly organized and easy for your website's visitors to quickly find the information most relevant to them.

URLs and Links

It's also important to have well-optimized page titles on your website. Using easy-to-understand titles that contain the keyword the page is designed for can get you a great head start in the rankings. Using links like www.mattthebuilder.com/home-extensions is far better than www.mattthebuilder.com/?id=321 both for search engines and real people.

The URL you choose for your website is also worth considering. Although it can seem logical to use the business name, this isn't always what potential customers will be searching for. It can be a good idea to use a descriptive name (and include your location if you're a local business) in your URL. Remember that you can always point additional URLs at your website

Planning and Writing

Next comes the planning and writing of the content for your website's pages. Remember to write with your keywords in mind, but not to sacrifice readability or usefulness to the humans who will be reading your pages. A website at the top of Google is useless (and won't stay top for long) if people don't find it useful and interesting, and you won't get the sale. Write in a friendly and personal style as if you were having a conversation with a potential client, customer or reader and remember to include your keywords and lots of variations as well as plenty of mentions of your location if you're a local business.

Including the keyword your page is designed for as a main heading is also a very good idea.

With any pictures used on the page, include your keyword as the Alt text.

You can also include Internal Links between your pages (links that direct people from one page to another, usually contained in the text). An example of a good use of internal links might be if you are listing the products or services that you offer, and you have specific pages about some of these products and services. When these products or services are mentioned, you can include a link to the right page.

Research shows that Google takes notice of the text used in internal links, so be sure to use the keywords each page is targeted at in any links you make, for example <a href="http://mattthebuilder.com/single-storey-extensions">Single Storey Extensions</a>, where 'Single Storey Extensions' is the anchor text (and target keyword).

Doing the promotion

Once your site is built, it's time to promote it like crazy. Google loves backlinks and by using the backlink finder at www.backlinkwatch.com you can find out how many backlinks your competitors have, and also where they come from.

You'll usually find that plenty of them come from directories and forums, and you can add these to your list of websites to target to get backlinks.

Submitting your website to directories is a great place to start collecting plenty of backlinks and there are literally thousands of directories out there from general directories of all websites, to specific local directories and specialist directories targeting a particular market or niche.

Be sure to complete your directory listings as fully as possible in order to make your entry stand out and get any preferential treatment that the directory might give to listings with high completion percentages. Including a website link is critical, and if you are a local business registered with Google Places it's a good idea to include your name, phone number and address exactly as it is shown on your Google Places listing as this will give it more weight and help to boost its ranking.

The next phase of your online promotion involves submitting articles written about your website, product or service to online article websites. As with directories, the quality of these websites can vary tremendously and it's a good idea to steer clear of spammy or poor quality sites as being associated with these can actually harm your Google ranking. Remember that in general the better the website you get an article published on, the more it will help your Google rank as well as attracting a targeted audience to your site.

Local news websites can be a fantastic place to get articles published, particularly if you are a local business, as they are usually pressed for stories and if you can offer them a well-written story about something that will be of interest to their readers, you have done all the hard work for them.

They also tend to be more likely to let you mention and link to your website more often. Try to use anchor text if they'll let you get away with it, but bear in mind that they will probably strip out any code before uploading the article to the website.
As for the content of your article, use your imagination! A story about your website might not be interesting enough to justify inclusion, but a story about the latest trends in X or the fashion amongst customers in Y probably will be, and might just be something that the publication wouldn't not be able to cover without your expertise. If the article proves a hit and they like it, don't be afraid to ask for a more regular spot which will give you much more exposure - and importantly, more back links!

Another great place to promote your website (subtley) is on forums relevant to your subject area. Many forums are extremely tight with their spam policies so might not allow new posters (or anyone for that matter) to post links, but by contributing to the forum over time you can begin to build a relationship with the other forum dwellers and will find natural places to mention your website.

If the forum allows posters to use links in their signatures, you have to exploit this opportunity and include a link (with keyword-rich anchor text) in your signature. Quite often, specialist forums will have a decent page rank so can be a great source of quality backlinks.

What's more is that this is one of those promotion strategies that not only helps your website out by building your Google listing, but also by driving targeted, quality traffic to your website.

Google+ Set up and Integration

Next, you'll want to set up and/or optimise your Google+ page. Start with your personal page and remember to add your website address to the list of links that you contribute to. Once you've done that, link back to your Google+ profile with a link from your site containing the rel=author tag we mentioned in the Authorship section.

Once your personal profile is ready, you'll want to set up a Google+ page for the website or business itself. In Google+ go to More->Pages then click to set up a page. Choose the right category (e.g. local place or business) and fill in as much of the info as you can. Remember to include pictures, description, hours of business as well as adding your website address and including a reciprocal link back from your website

If your business has a physical address and this is relevant (i.e. you are a local business and want to show up in local results) it's also worth Verifying your business by asking Google to send you a postcard at your address. Once your page is verified, you will be eligible to show up with an address block in the search results. More information about this is available in my Google Places guide.

Ongoing Promotion

Google likes to see a steady stream of promotion for your website and SEO isn't really something that you can 'set or forget', so my advice would be to set aside half an hour per week to promote your website online in as many targeted places you can find.

Once you have run out of forums and directories relevant to your area, you can try asking suppliers, customers and other local/relevant websites to link to your website. You'll be surprised how many people will agree if you just ask.

Also remember to update your website as often as you can by adding new content. A great way to make this really easy is to start a blog on your site. Here you can write about anything that interests you which will also be of value to your website visitors. It's never easy to start, but once you're started with a blog you'll find it much easier to get into the swing of things.

Google loves websites that are updated frequently, and the more frequently your website is updated, the more often Google's spiders will crawl and index it.

If you run a Twitter and/or Facebook page, remember to tweet/link to your latest blog posts as this helps to increase the number of links to your website as well as directing a good flow of visitors.

If you have implemented the testimonial rich text snippets, you'll also want to keep these as up-to-date as possible. The date of the most recent testimonial will show up in the Google search results and we know from experimentation that searchers will be more likely to click on webpages that have been updated most recently.

Further Help and Information

I'd like to thank you for reading this guide and I sincerely hope that it has been useful to you. A lot of website owners pay good money to have these strategies implemented for them, and I think it's important that you understand exactly what it takes to get to the top of Google, because it is so important.

Hopefully you can see that while it's not *easy* to rank number 1, and some markets are certainly tougher than others - for example banking, mortgages or anything where you are competing with £50,000+ per month SEO teams - the tasks involved are actually relatively simple and a large portion of the work is simply building a readable website, making it useful to people and then promoting it.

If, having seen what is involved in getting a website to the top of Google, you have decided that you would like some help with some or all of your SEO work then I am happy to talk with you about taking it on so you can get on with running the business. My company Exposure Ninja (http://exposureninja.com) builds websites and provides SEO and online promotion for businesses, whether local or national.

Throughout this book I have sung the praises of Wordpress as a website building tool and if you are yet to build a website or would like to take control of your own website, I cannot recommend it highly enough. Wordpress is free to use and quite simple once you know your way around, although the initial set up can be a little complicated if you are new to FTP. I have a course showing you exactly how to set up and maintain a Wordpress site which you will find more details about at www.Get2TheTopOfGoogle.com/offers

If you are a local business and would like more information about Google Places, and how to get your listing ranking more highly, I also have a guide giving you step by step information on how to do this. Again, more details are at www.Get2TheTopOfGoogle.com/offers

How To Get To The Top Of Google+ Local/Google Places

Tim Kitchen
www.Get2TheTopOfGoogle.com

Table of Contents

Introduction

Why this book exists

In April 2012, the first edition of 'How to Get to The Top of Google' hit the stores and was instantly way more popular than I could have hoped. The feedback was great and it wasn't long before the success stories started coming in.

But by far the biggest request was for more information about Google Places, Google Maps, Google Local and the various names and products Google uses to try to capture and present information about our local area. Everyone from car mechanics to electricians, musicians and florists wanted to know how to show up on that map on the front page of Google. So I realized I needed to answer this question.

The effect of Google Places on local business

For marketers and owners of local businesses, Google Places is one of the biggest opportunities to attract new customers since Google's dominance of the search engine world began.

It's still not uncommon to see unclaimed or poorly optimised Places listings with great placement at the top of the page, listed above well-optimised and heavily backlinked *regular* websites, which are shown further down the page. Worse still, some local businesses found their websites had been bumped onto page 2 as a result of the increase in the number of Places results shown on the Search Engine Results Page (SERP). Sometimes there are as few as 4 regular listings on a page because of the number of Places results, so it's not hard to see why savvy businesses and SEOs are really starting to focus on the relatively new field of Places/+Local optimisation.

The truth is that getting to the top of Google Places can be a phenomenal shortcut and alternative to more traditional SEO and competing with well-optimised and professional websites.

With Google Places, Google is attempting to cement their service as the 'go to' destination for people who need the services of a local business. By showing phone numbers and addresses for the Places results, customers who are quickly looking for contact or location info aren't required to click through to the business website.

This is all part of Google's plan. As we've seen with Google images, stock prices, translations, definitions, exchange rates and many other set definable requests ("$48 in £" or "weather today in Bristol" for example), Google is gradually adopting a new role: rather than simply gathering data it thinks might be relevant, it's beginning to make choices and dig a little deeper in order to provide the exact information required direct to the searcher, without them even having to visit the website.

This shift away from simply providing a list of websites that might be of interest to actually giving the searcher the information they require might seem subtle at first, but its impact on the web is yet to be fully realized.

As many local business owners are coming to understand, having a good well-optimised website is no longer enough in many markets. Playing by Google's rules and jumping through their hoops is more important than ever, and Google Places and +Local is the latest hoop smart business owners are crowding to jump through.

Google Places vs Google+ for Business vs Google+ Local vs Google Maps

As I write this (in October 2012) the naming and organization of Google's various local products is somewhat unclear. And by 'somewhat unclear' I mean pretty much you'd have to be running the local division of Google in order to understand what the hell is going on.

We are in a transition phase as Google begins to integrate what was Places into its Google+ product. Currently, business owners can still manage their business listings through Google Places, but over time Google Places will become Google+ Local.

For *consumers,* Google+ Local is the product they use to find local businesses, read reviews and do all they used to do in Google Places, but confusingly if they use Google maps, they are seeing Places results.

Added to that, if you are a Google+ user who also owns a business, you can set up a Google+ for Business page. As the name would suggest, this is a Google+ page specifically for your business. It also contains local information and over time Google will be merging + for Business and + Local pages into one.

Google Maps is still Google Maps. The results that show up in Google Maps results and on the front page of Google in the map results and 7-pack are Google+ Local results *and* Places results.

If this sounds confusing, it is. Sorry.

In the interests of clarity and being as future proof as possible, for the majority of the rest of this guide I will no longer refer to the soon-to-be-extinct Google Places, but instead Google+ Local. We will look briefly at Google Places, but its time is limited, so too much focus is not necessary.
With all that cleared up (...) let's get stuck in!

How to Look at Google+ Local

The truth is that the local results that Google displays are just another type of search result. Because of this, many of the standard SEO (Search Engine Optimisation, or 'trying to improve ranking') best practices apply, albeit with small modifications.

So in order to best understand exactly what's going on with Google+ Local, and how to apply our existing knowledge of what makes a well-optimised listing in Google's *regular* organic results, we need a framework which we can use. Think of this framework as the language dictionary that helps us translate best practice from regular SEO to our new language of Google+ Local.

The truth is, that while no one knows exactly what algorithm Google is using for either their regular results or + Local results, far more is known about how to manipulate and 'optimise' for the regular results than the newer (and in many cases more important) + Local results.

By establishing this framework, we can tap into the understandings of SEO and use them to get Local success.

Regular Google Results

So first let's look at the most commonly accepted 'rules' of regular Search Engine Optimisation. It's worth noting that while each of the following are important, it is not always necessary to have *all* of these factors highly optimised in order to get great results. Also please note that this book is not a guide on regular SEO, but it's helpful to revisit the basic principles in order to understand what's going on inside the + Local algorithm and how to boost our rankings.

1) Keyword matching. It's obvious that when you search for "New Cars Croydon", Google is going to be returning websites that feature the phrase (and individual words) "new cars Croydon". These words known as 'keywords' have always been the foundation of Google's search. Keywords can be used in different places to serve different purposes, for example:
    a. In the website's title. This is a great place to start and makes it obvious for Google what the webpage's content is focused on. A page called 'New Cars in Croydon' is likely to be pretty well-targeted to our "new cars Croydon" searcher above.
    b. In the content of the web page. Again, when Google is crawling the webpage, the more instances of the keyword it finds, the safer it is to assume that the page will be of interest to someone searching that particular phrase.
    c. In the URL of the website. This is an incredibly powerful way of shortcutting a lot of regular SEO, and has been responsible for many of my literally 'overnight' successes. By using the exact keyphrase as the URL of the website, you can get the site showing up in SERPs before it's even been fully indexed by Google. This effect has started to wane slightly after some very recent Google updates, but it's still powerful for high quality (non-spammy) websites. It's also worth noting that by using decent link structure (e.g. www.newcars.com/new-cars/croydon rather than www.newcars.com/2012/pa-265.html) you are using more keywords in your URL whilst at the same time making it simpler for your visitors to understand what your pages will be about.
    d. In anchor text of links to your site, whether from other websites or from different places on your website. Anchor text is the text that makes up the link pointing to your site, for example the

classically useless click here. There's overwhelming evidence that Google places extremely high importance on the words used in this anchor text when deciding the relevance of a website, so it makes sense to use good, relevant and keyword-rich anchor text in all your links.

For an interesting example, Google "click here". You'll see that the top result is the webpage for Adobe Reader. The reason it has such excellent ranking for this phrase, despite not actually using this phrase on the page itself, is because of the millions of "To view this PDF you'll need Adobe Reader. To get Adobe Reader, click here" links all over the internet. This gives us an insight into the importance of anchor text in Google's eyes, that it would rank a website so high for this phrase, even if the site makes *no mention* of that phrase at all.

2) Backlinking. In order for Google to show searchers the most relevant results possible, it likes to know which websites are the most popular. That way it can be sure that when you type in "Wal Mart" you get the Wal Mart website rather than a forum discussing Wal Mart. Although the Wal Mart forum might have more mentions of the phrase "wal mart" than the Wal Mart homepage, it is not as popular a page as the retail giant's own. One of the ways Google measures popularity is by seeing how many times each page is mentioned or linked to by other pages on the Internet. These links are known as backlinks. What's more is that Google gives each website a popularity score, known as Pagerank. In Google's eyes, a link from a high Pagerank (more important) website is worth more than a link from a low Pagerank (less important) website. Think of it like this: if all the cool kids are talking about you, you *must* be cool too.
3) Structure and size of the website. Another important factor is that your website *works*. That is there are no

broken pages and it's not just a simple one-page job but has plenty of content for interested searchers to quench their thirst. Remember that Google is simply doing its best to try and imitate human preferences. When you are looking for some information, you are likely to be more impressed by a website that has lots of relevant info versus a site that has a few lines of info stuffed full of the keyword and offering nothing original. The Google bots also need to be able to 'crawl' your website and find their way around, so making sure that you have simple navigation is a good idea. People should be able to find the information they want from your site within a couple of clicks at most, and it should be intuitive where to look.

4) Time on site and bounce rate. When Google shows your website in the results page, it's taking a gamble: "will this person be grateful to me for showing them this website? Or will they leave dissatisfied and go over to Bing" OK it might not be *that* extreme, but nonetheless Google wants to know that the results it's serving up are being valued by its searchers. One of the ways it judges this is by measuring the time visitors spend on your site, and the number that immediately 'bounce back' to the Google results page. Please note, I'm not talking about Google Analytics here, I'm talking about the Google search engine noticing how fast visitors return back to the search after visiting a link. On the whole, spending a short time on the website is a sign that it wasn't very interesting, useful or relevant, and Google will want to know this information. The best way to keep visitors on your website immediately with very little effort is to put up a short video. The video can be 30 seconds long and could just be a quick promo video made on animoto (www.animoto.com) or another similar site. The point is that once a visitor clicks on your site and sees a video, they're likely to watch it. If the video is 1 minute long, you have just increased the average time on your site by 1 minute for everyone who watches the video

So those are the basics behind regular SEO.

How Google+ Local and Regular Google Results Fit Together

My experience running around 50 local websites for clients in different industries is this: the best results come when you do *both* regular SEO and Google+ Local optimisation.

If you do *only* regular SEO, then even if your website ranks highly, it could still be stuck at the bottom of the page below the local results. At the same time, if you only set up a Google+ Local page and skip having your own website, not only will you find it harder to rank on the maps results but you'll also find it *much* harder to convert local traffic into customers. In my experience, visitors still want to see a website. Just having your name and number show up at the top of Google is not enough - surfers want information about you before they pick up the phone. With the amount of choice available to online searchers, you really need to be showing your best in order to get their business.

Ideal Results

So the approach I'm going to prescribe in this guide is a hybrid of regular SEO and Google+ Local Optimisation and promotion.

It's the approach which has got me numerous first place listings in both + Local results and also the + local/website hybrid results. These results are my favourite because they really dominate a page: as well as your regular website listing, a pin and address block is visible which can also be seen on the map.

I've included a screenshot of what I mean below:

As you can see, this 'super listing' is the result of a combination SEO and + Local approach which gives the website great position but also adds the local element.

(In case you're wondering about the effect of this sort of result, this listing has literally changed the client's life. To see the testimonial, head over to my website http://exposureninja.com).

The sort of result above requires a lot of time and patience. The work for this listing was done almost a year ago and only in the past 6 months has the +Local integration started to be visible.

Although I recommend a solid SEO campaign to go alongside a Google+ Local/Google Places campaign, this book will focus on only the local element. The regular SEO side is covered by my book "How to Get to the Top of Google", available on Kindle or through http://get2thetopofgoogle.com

Google+ Local – First Steps

Your Personal Google+ Page

The first step to take is to sign up for Google+. Before setting up or claiming a business page, I'd recommend setting up a personal profile. Head over to http://plus.google.com and click the SIGN UP button. If you already have a Google account, you can instead just sign in with your regular username and password and you will be guided through the process of upgrading your profile to Google+.

As mentioned in my book 'How to Get to the Top of Google', there are advantages to being on Google+ from an SEO point of view, and little tricks like using authorship markup can be really powerful in boosting your website's visibility. But that side of things is covered in more detail in that book and we are primarily concerned with the local element here so simply fill out your profile as completely as possible, adding pictures, descriptions, links... the whole works.

Creating Your Google+ Local Page

Once your personal Google+ profile is complete, on the left hand side of the page you'll see a menu. It looks like it's greyed out, but in fact that's just Google's (somewhat confusing) style. Go to More and hover the mouse over it until the Pages option appears, then click it.

Next, click the link to Create New Page and choose the relevant category. If you're a local business (a pretty safe bet considering the subject of this book!), then the first option 'Local Business or Place' is the one to choose.

You will now be asked to enter your primary phone number, as this is how Google identifies if you already have a listing set up (whether someone did it manually or it was automatically created in the Places days). Remember that the goal is to find existing listings if they exist - we don't want to create duplicate listings if we can at all help it, trust me!

Once you enter your phone number, Google will present you with any businesses that match. If there are no matches, you will be taken through to enter your address and the details of your business. If you find that your business *is* already listed, you can click to confirm the address and category before clicking to Create the Page.

Creating a Google Places listing

In addition to a Google+ Local listing, currently you can still create a Google Places listing for your business. Although Google is in the process of merging these two products, if you have the option to create both then you should.

To add your Google Places listing, visit www.google.com/local/add

You will be taken through the process step-by-step of adding your local listing and remember to fill in each section as thoroughly as possible, including pictures and especially a link to your website.

Also make sure that your business name, address and phone number are listed exactly the same as on your website and on your Google+ local page. This is really important!

Later on we'll take a look at some more Google Places loveliness (including building and embedding a map of your business location on your website) but for now we're going to return to the more current world of Google+ Local.

How is my business already listed?

When Google was building its Google Places product, it scraped business information from numerous places in order to create listings for many local businesses automatically. Then once Google Places became Google+ Local, these listings were upgraded to the new format. The result is that many businesses already have Google+ Local listings, even if they didn't manually add them.

Google has been known to punish those who set up duplicate listings, so best to stay on the safe side.

The Phone Number and Google+ Local

It's worth stopping for a moment to talk about the role of the phone number in the world of Google+ Local.

What we've actually *just seen* is a pretty significant insight, I believe, into the workings of Google+ Local and there are some significant implications for ranking.

We've just seen how Google identifies a business by its phone number (particularly local landline numbers). There was no request for address, website or even business name. All that was required was a phone number. This makes sense if you consider that many businesses don't have websites, some will share names and often one building will house many businesses. But phone numbers are nearly always unique to the business.

I've long held the view that a phone number is to Google+ Local what a website address is to regular Google. It's a unique identifier for that business. In other words the phone number is the thing you promote, the thing you get listed, the thing that Google looks at to judge popularity.

This is where my experience of regular SEO and + Local SEO really start to converge: the strategy I use for my clients is to promote their Google+ Local listing in the same way as I promote their websites but rather than use a web address to link, I'll use a citation. (Citations are basically a listing of a business's name, address and phone number. I personally believe the phone number is responsible for nearly all of the effect, but it does no harm to include the whole citation. We'll look at citations in more detail later on).

Profile Basics

As with everything Google+ you'll want to fill in the details of your profile as completely as possible, and that includes adding a profile photo. Unlike your personal Google+ page, this doesn't necessarily have to be a head shot of you and can be a logo, picture of your premises or something else relevant. If you don't have a suitable picture just yet you can add one later, but it is advisable to add one.

You'll be offered the choice to promote your page on your personal Google+ profile and this is optional.

The next step is to start filling in the publicly visible information. You'll see a button at the top of the screen to Edit Profile and this will allow you to write an introduction, put in your hours of business, add additional phone numbers, link to your website and also put in some other links of interest. This can be a good place to link to any promotional videos you have or other sites relevant to your business.

You can also add photos and videos to your page, and this is advisable. Remember that the more complete the profile, the better.

Linking Your Website

If you have a website and have linked to it in your About section, you'll see a button appear to link this website to your Google+ Local page. To do this, all you need to do is click the button, copy the text that appears and have this embedded somewhere on your website's homepage. This step is absolutely crucial because it's what allows Google to verify that the website and Google+ Local page are associated so that they can display the Google+ Local information alongside the website in search results, as seen earlier.

To be clear, linking your website to your Google+ Local page doesn't *guarantee* that Google will show address information next to your website in the search results, it just makes it possible. Unfortunately Google likes to take its time in approving such linking, but nevertheless this is one of the most important steps to take in boosting your Google+ Local visibility.

Verifying Your Google+ Local Listing

The next step is also crucial for ensuring that you are visible in local searches. You'll notice that your Google+ Local page is labeled 'Unverified'. This means that Google hasn't seen verification that you, the person responsible for editing the page, is in actual fact the business owner.

In order to verify the page, Google needs to confirm your address. By clicking the button Verify Now, you can ask Google to send a postcard through to your business address containing a PIN number. Once you get this postcard, you can head back to your Google+ Local page and type it in to verify your listing.

The postcard usually takes around 10 days to arrive in the UK. If after a couple weeks it still hasn't arrived, you can request another to be sent out. But this step is really important so I'd recommend not putting it off or ignoring it.

Again, once you've entered your PIN, there will be a wait while Google confirms the verification. How long depends on how Google is feeling, and there's nothing you or I can do about it.

Just as we do for regular SEO, I'm going to break down the components of a successful Google+ Local promotion campaign into 2 categories: on-listing and off-listing.

On-Listing Strategies

Just like On-page optimisation in regular SEO, on-listing strategies in Google+ Local are things we can do to the listing itself in order to help it rank higher.

Business Name

Your business name should be real, in other words it should be what you call your business. The temptation might be to stuff your business title with lots of juicy keywords: "Cutting Edge Hair, Hair salon in Chichester, bridal hair, wedding hair, L'Oreal colour specialists."

This is frowned upon by the big G who understandably doesn't want to see the + Local results become overrun with keyword spam in the way that regular search results have in the past.

However, what I suggest to many of my one-man band clients is that unless they already have an established brand awareness in their town, they might consider choosing a more 'optimised' name for their business.

Let's take the local plumber as a typical example. Many plumbers will, without hesitation, call their companies after themselves: Barry White Plumbing & Heating Services. This is fine, but actually unless Barry is well-known in the area, there are more suitable names that could get him showing up higher in Google.

If Barry is based in Leicester for example, he might choose to call himself Leicester Plumbing & Heating. This is going to more closely match what people search for, as well as give him a bit more credibility when he does show up in the search results. While it's not advised to add extra keywords to a business name, in some cases you can rename the business to contain keywords. This is perfectly acceptable and has been responsible for some of my clients making a ridiculously large return on investment on our local marketing services.
But I know that it's not always possible. If you're a shop or have an established website already and a sneaky change of name isn't practical, then don't be tempted to add extra keywords in the name field. Don't worry, there are plenty of other things we can do…

Phone and Email

It's obviously important that the phone number on the Google+ Local listing is correct, and where possible this should be a geographic landline because Google can use this to locate the business in a particular area and it is another reassuring sign of a 'genuine' business. For my clients that have multiple offices or want to serve multiple locations, I recommend setting up different regional phone numbers through a service like Voipfone which can all be directed to one number or their mobile.
You can add email addresses to your Google+ Local profile in the Contact Info section where your phone numbers are displayed. Simply choose Email from the dropdown box. Email addresses should, if possible, be from your website's domain, i.e. barry@leicesterplumbingandheating.com rather than sparklefairy69@hotmail.co.uk. Ask yourself 'if Google was trying to see which option represented a more legitimate business, which would they choose?'

Description

The Introduction section on your Google+ Local profile serves 2 purposes:

1) To give visitors an insight into what you do
2) To give Google an insight into what you do.

So you want to make sure that you're primary keyphrases (the phrases you want to show up for) are included in this introduction, but try to include them in a classy, refined way rather than sounding spammy or unnatural. It's worth mentioning the areas you serve as well as any variations of your keyphrases that describe your product or service. Don't be afraid of writing a lot of text here, and you can also link to specific pages on your website (for example: "we have a large customer base in Leicester, and our testimonials from past plumbing customers are extremely important to us). Here you included a link with good anchor text as well as your location and service.

Photos

Adding photos is a very good idea to create a more complete profile that is more likely to convert potential visitors. It also shows Google that you are putting in the effort, and if Google has the choice between showing an incomplete profile and one with loads of photos… you get the idea!

Videos

The same can be said about videos although unfortunately Google actually requires you to upload videos to the page, whereas before in Google Places you could simply link to them from YouTube.

Reviews

Reviews: everyone's favourite. With Google+ Local, Google has joined forces with Zagat, a local review service. Zagat has a rather confusing scoring system with a maximum of 30. The result of this is that a 26 in a red box looks at first glance like a very poor score out of 100, whereas actually it's considered a very *good* score.

To confuse matters further, reviews from the old Google Places still show up, but without scores and are attributed to the anonymous sounding 'A Google User'.

Reviews used to be aggregated from other sites as well, such as Thomson Local, Qype and others, but whilst you can still click to see reviews left on other sites, they are not automatically displayed on the Google+ Local page and they don't contribute to overall rating. This is a real source of annoyance for businesses that for years focussed on these other platforms to build an excellent base of reviews that are now virtually invisible, whilst their Google+ Local page lies barren and review-less.

But anyway, the Google Local reviews system has been the target for various attempts to manipulate and create false reviews to boost rankings. As a result of this, Google is unable to be so straightforward as to rank local listings in order of best reviews – the system is too open to manipulation.

But it does help to have *some* reviews, and the best place to have them is actually on your Google+ Local page.

Rather than writing your own reviews, you can take two approaches:

- Ask your customers to leave you reviews. Many of them won't bother and many of the ones that do will be unable to figure out how to do it
- Head over to the internet in search of buying reviews.

I recommend the first approach, but if you did want to experiment with the second you might want to look in the direction of Fiverr and Amazon's Mechanical Turk, which is a platform for recruiting people from around the world to perform small tasks very cheaply.
You might be wondering why you can't just sign up for multiple Google accounts and leave the reviews yourself. The reason why this doesn't work is because Google specializes in tracking you. Short of using a different computer, on a different network, with different sign up details for each new account, they will eventually find you out. I've personally tried IP blockers, VPNs, clean cache, disabled cookies, parallels installations with different MAC addresses… the lot. They find you. Honestly it's just easier to ask customers to leave reviews while you get on with the other promotion.
So those are the on-listing strategies to get your Google+ Local profile fully optimised and ready to go.

Off-listing factors

Just like regular SEO works on the basis of links and website addresses, local SEO is about citations and your business's *physical* address. When promoting your Google+ Local website, you should aim to get your **n**ame, **a**ddress and **p**hone number (NAP for short) listed in as many relevant places as possible.

Directories

Just like regular SEO, targeted directories and local websites are a great place to start.

But first a warning about directories: many people new to SEO and +Local optimisation will assume that if a few directories is good, then more must be better. They sign up to every directory site under the sun - even the low quality spammy ones, and a bunch that really aren't relevant to their target market. The problem with this approach is that if you do it enough you can raise flags with Google who sees people appearing on these low quality spammy directories as spammers.
The Holy Grail for directory listings are directories that are curated and an actual human being sorts through the new listings and approves them. Ideally you want your directories to be quite difficult to get into, because that keeps the spammers away. Failing that, at least make sure they have a fairly lengthly sign up process (like Freeindex or Yelp for example).
With that said, let's look at the best sorts of directories to target.

Local Area Directories

The first is local directories in our area. If you Google "<your area> business directory", you will usually find a few local business directories specifically targeted to your area. These are fantastic because they're generally kept quite small and relevant and aren't overrun by spam. They're also a good source of local traffic for your website and + Local listing too, so as well as the citation you are more likely to pick up some potential customers. Google likes them because they are *relevant* due to their local focus.

As with all directory listings, try to complete your entry as fully as possible and include pictures if you can. All of these directory sites want their listings to be as complete as possible and potential customers will be more likely to click on you if they can see pictures. In order to boost your +Local page, you can also link directly to it from each directory listing as well. If the listing allows you to enter more than one website address, as well as your main website link, you can add a link to your +Local page. If the directory doesn't allow more than one link, then you can often add a link in the description and where possible make it a live clickable link.

I also like to include a full NAP citation in the description where possible, shown in the exact format used on the Google+ Local page. Many local SEOs claim that

Market Specific Directories

The next category of directories you should target is market-specific directories. To find these, simply search for "<your business type> directory", e.g. "funeral director directory". List yourself in as many of these as possible as long as they are good quality and not filled with spam. After the recent Google updates, it's pretty unlikely that spam-ridden directories will be easily findable, but it's still possible so use your judgement and ask: 'does this look like a quality directory I would trust?' Again it's good practice to include a link to your Google+ Local page in these directory listings because this it will be highly targeted and relevant as a result of the single business category focus of the directory.

High Quality National Directories

The next category of directories is the good quality national business directories. These are sites like Yelp, Qype, Freeindex, Yell, Thomson Local and Scoot (which populates the Sun and the Independent - a very high ranking directory!). These directories are amongst those favoured by Google because they generally require some level of approval or have a more complicated signup process (for example, my Indian team is unable to sign up to Yelp – it has to be done manually by me or someone else in the UK).

Recommended Directories (UK)

My current favourites for UK-based businesses are:
www.qype.co.uk
www.yelp.co.uk
www.fyple.co.uk
www.hotfrog.co.uk
http://freeindex.co.uk
www.uksmallbusinessdirectory.co.uk
http://directory.independent.co.uk
http://listings.touchlocal.com
www.smilelocal.com
www.misterwhat.co.uk
www.city-visitor.com
www.brownbook.net
www.thomsonlocal.com
www.ufindus.com
www.yell.com
www.tipped.co.uk

Many of these have international versions too, and if you want to find more here's how: search for your product or service, then go through the Google results pages identifying all the directories that are showing up. Now you know which are the most authoritative in Google's eyes, you can start listing yourself in them.

As mentioned before - complete these listings as fully as possible. Sometimes verification is required before the listing can be fully completed and it can be tempting to skip the final step if this verification takes a couple days. Don't do it! The difference between a fully complete directory listing and a half-assed quick basics job is probably 10 minutes, max. The best 10 minutes you can spend.

Also remember to link to your Google+ Local page and include a full NAP citation, if the directory allows it.

Other Sources of Citations

Because citations of the business's Name Address and Phone number (NAP) are important for getting great + Local rank, it's worth exploring some other places we can put these citations that Google will index.

If you have a Twitter account, consider adding a citation to your Twitter description. Remember you can also link to your Google+ Local page from your Twitter account, which can be great if your Twitter account is active and you are regularly posting relevant messages that are interesting to your target market.

The same goes for Facebook. Many small businesses set up a local business page expecting it to drive hundreds of 'viral' customers to their business. OK so that's not going to happen, but at least we can use your Facebook page to drive juicy high quality links and citations at your business. Include your NAP listing in the same format as seen on your Google+ Local page, and add a link to the page itself as well as your main website.

For our local clients, we usually set up a YouTube channel and post a few short, very simple promotional videos. In the description for each of these videos we will add a NAP citation as well as a link back to their website. Then from the channel description we'll add another citation with links to the website and + Local page included in the relevant channel links section.

All of these social citations build up the number of citations Google is likely to index, and make high +Local rank far more likely.

If you can get business partners, suppliers or customers to link to your website from theirs and include a NAP citation, that's a good source of quality links. It's far better than spamming blogs or linking in poor quality directories because (hopefully) the site will be higher quality and more relevant to your business, market or location.

Guest blogging can be a shortcut to getting in front of a large audience, and whenever you write for another website it's good practice to include a link and NAP citation, not only increasing your rank and number of citations but also increasing the chances that visitors who enjoyed the article will become customers down the line.

It's beyond the scope of this Google+ Local guide to show you how to set up guest blogging relationships, but there are plenty of guides out there about this.

On-Website Factors

We'll now look at some things you can do on your website itself in order to boost your Google+ Local profile, as well as increase conversions of local visitors.

Google maps on linked website

One of the key issues with local website visitors is trust. People often feel more comfortable using a business that is close to them, because they feel a stronger connection and a safety that if something goes horrendously wrong with their purchase, they can go round and get it fixed.

But even for businesses that aren't close by, knowing that they have a physical location makes them seem far more accountable. And nothing says 'physical location' like a map saying "we are here"!

To add a map showing your business location, first sign into Google and head over to google.com/maps. Now you'll need to find your business on the map (please note that you must have set up your Google Places listing already and verified your address through the Places postcard. Please also note that the Places postcard is different to the +Local postcard, and usually takes about a week longer to arrive. Yes I know, Google don't make it easy do they).

Once you have found your business listing on Google maps (try finding your area, searching for your business name and clicking on the red dot marker if your business isn't yet showing up in the results on the left hand side), click on its map location and you'll see more information pop up. You'll also see a link to 'Save to Map'. Click this and select 'Create a new map' from the drop down box, then hit Save. Your new map has then been created and it's time to edit it and make it a little more useful for your website visitors. Click Edit on your map page and you'll get the ability to write a Title and Description. Remember to use your keywords & phrases in these descriptions, but also to make them relevant and useful as they will be displayed anywhere you embed this new map (like on your website).

Once you are happy with your title and description, click Save.

The next step is to get the code for this map so that we can embed it on our website. Obviously this step requires that you have access to the code of your website (and that you have a website). If you don't and would like to, feel free to get in touch with me through www.exposureninja.com.

To get the embed code, simply click the button above Save that looks like chain links. You'll then be shown 2 pieces of code - 1 for a link and the second to embed the map. If you like you can customise the map (I usually shrink them down a bit) by clicking the Customise link, and once you are happy you can copy the embed code. You can now paste this code anywhere on your site and your visitors will see your business displayed on a map.

As well as being great for your visitors, you now have another link to your business location specifically in a Google friendly format. Awesome.

Links to Your Google+ Local (and Places) Page

As part of your verification of your Google+ Local page, you will have included a link from your website back to this page. But if, like me, you put this link quite small in the footer of the website, it can also be a good idea to include a larger and more visible link on another page of your site. In the next chapter we will be looking at getting reviews for your business on your +Local page, and once you have some quality reviews it can be beneficial to send website visitors over to your +Local page to have a look at these reviews. For that reason, for businesses that are more active in collecting reviews or who use the Google+ Local pages more often, I'll put a link back to their profile on the Contact or Testimonials page of their website.

On-Site Citations

As well as having lots of juicy NAP citations on directories, social media and other websites, it's a great idea to double check that your location details and phone number are 100% correct and visible on every page of your website. You wouldn't believe the number of local businesses who bury their address - or even forget to include it all together - on their websites, expecting all potential customers to pick up the phone.

If you're technically-minded, the best format for your NAP citations on your website is the hCard format. This is a Google-readable special piece of code that identifies your location information as a sort of virtual business card, and allows Google to display it accordingly in the search results. (Currently I haven't seen Google do anything special with the hCard information yet, although other rich snippet text *is* treated differently, so it's likely that at some point in the future this will happen).

If you're running Wordpress, I recommend the Customer Reviews plugin as it allows both the hCard info to be shown on every page of your website as well as displaying your customer reviews in hReview format which can lead to the gold stars showing in your Google results page listings. Very cool (and free). For more info, see my other book How to Get to the Top of Google.

Other Factors

Phone Numbers

When trying to show up in a certain area, it's most desirable (both from a Google point of view and a potential customer's point of view) to have a local phone number. The area code should ideally match your target area, but any landline is better than no landline.

If you are a purely mobile business, then one thing you can do is set up a virtual landline from a website like www.voipfone.com. Services like Voipfone allow you to set up a local phone number with an area code of your choice that you can redirect either to your computer, or to another phone - including mobiles.

If you have a number of regional offices each with their own address and phone number, then I recommend setting up different Google+ Local & Places accounts for each one and using their own local numbers. Not only will this give you more locations visible, but it will also make each listing better optimised and as a result more likely to get great ranking.

Proximity to Location

One inescapable fact is that if you are not based near your target location, it is going to be very difficult for you to rank really highly in the local results. For example, one of my clients installs bathrooms. Because he lives in a tiny village miles from anywhere, we decided that it would be best to target his nearest big city so we set up a well-optimised website, Places and +Local pages for him. Although he rarely shows up as a Places result in local search for that city (because he is located about 20 miles outside it), we optimised his site well enough with regular SEO that he gets fantastic Google rank with his combined website *and* local listing.

So in cases where you are at a disadvantage against your competitors due to your distance from your target market, you might want to focus more intensely on regular SEO.

It used to be that those who were closest to the very centre of the location pin in a particular place stood the best chance of ranking well. Over time we've seen this effect start to dilute slightly, and now you'll notice that it is not the closest businesses to a particular location that necessarily show up, but the best optimised/most popular/most citations that win. Of course as in the example above, business located far outside a location are still at a disadvantage, but it is no longer necessary to be dead centre in order to rank well.

Age of Listing

While having a mature listing isn't necessarily a guarantee for success, brand new listings will be less likely to rank highly early on. Typically I tell clients to allow 4-6 months before the full effect of Google+ Local/Places work has taken effect. During this time I'll run adwords ads for them to get some early traffic and get things moving, and make sure that the pages have been verified properly and PINs submitted as soon as we get them.

Duplicate Listings

For those who already have a Google listing but it hasn't yet been claimed, the temptation can be to 'start again' and create a new listing from scratch. This is against Google's policies though, and as such is inadvisable. Trust me, if I thought you could get ahead this way I'd be advocating it, but in reality the maturity of your existing listing will be much more useful to you that a duplicate listing which could risk your removal entirely.

For this reason, it's always advisable to try and find any existing listings you have when signing up - even if you have to check alternative phone numbers to find them.

If you do accidentally create a duplicate listing, it's best to remove the new one and instead optimise the old one and make sure it is up to scratch.

Summary

As Google continues to improve and enhance its search to take into consideration location, social signals and intent, it will be more and more important to 'play ball' with Google's new products and services. Google+ Local and Places is the current best option for local businesses looking to get exposure with searchers in the local area, and hopefully the contents of this guide will help you get started in this relatively new field.

The key aspects of a successful Google Local placement:

- Google+ Local page, well optimised, linked to website and with address verified
- Google Places page, well optimised, address verified and with website link
- Relevant and local directory listings
- Properly optimised website with location, Google map and hCard address information if possible
- Article writing, guest blogging and having other relevant sites link to yours including a NAP citation as well as your website link
- Publicising your Google+ page and encouraging your customers to leave reviews, as this will improve your conversions and lead to more traffic for your page

I hope you've enjoyed this guide and that you are now able to go forth and put these strategies into place. If you need to get in touch my email is tim@timkitchen.com or alternatively you can get through to me through my company's website http://exposureninja.com

Go forth and dominate!

Tim K

KEYWORDS

nanny - nannies - Full time - Daily - Live
- part time - temporary - overseas nan
Areas of London / Hampshire / Dorset / Berkshire et
rotation -
Childcare - Nanny payroll - DBS certificate -
1st Aid Certificate - Norland -

15236557R00083

Printed in Great Britain
by Amazon.co.uk, Ltd.,
Marston Gate.